Forgiveness

An Invitation
to Freedom

Cindy,
May God bless your life
and may your always
be forgiven + be forgiving.

Bill Carpenter

Forgiveness
An Invitation
to Freedom

William E. Carpenter, D.Min.

Ann O. Slimp, PhD.

 MMRi Publishing
Suwanee, Georgia

Forgiveness
An Invitation
to Freedom

Copyright © 2005
MMRi Publishing
First Printing 2005

Unless otherwise indicated, Scripture quotations are from the New Revised Standard
Version of the Bible, copyright © 1989 by the Division of Christian Education of the
National Council of Churches of Christ in the U.S.A., and are used by permission.

Scripture quotations marked NIV are taken from the HOLY BIBLE: NEW
INTERNATIONAL VERSION. Copyright © 1973, 1978, 1984 by the International
Bible Society. Used by permission of Zondervan Bible Publishers.

Scripture quotations marked NASB are taken from the NEW AMERICAN
STANDARD BIBLE®, © Copyright 1960, 1962, 1963, 1968, 1971, 1972, 1973, 1975,
1977, 1995 by The Lockman Foundation. Used by permission.

Psalm 91 from Psalms/Now © 1973 Concordia Publishing House.
Used with permission. All rights reserved.

Published by:
MMRi Publishing
1000 Peachtree Industrial Boulevard
Suite 6 – 309
Suwanee, Georgia 30024
www.mmri.info

ISBN 0-9766293-0-5

1. Forgiveness—Religious aspects—Christianity. I. Title.

Printed in the USA by

MP

Morris Publishing
3212 East Highway 30 – Kearney, NE 68847 – 1-800-650-7888

*Forgiveness is
the fragrance
the violet sheds
on the heel
that has crushed it.*

Mark Twain

Table of Contents

Acknowledgements

We want to thank our families for their support during the writing of the manuscript, and especially Gayle Dean Carpenter and Kevin Slimp. For Gayle's time and attention to detail in editing many drafts of this book and Kevin's creativity and expertise in designing the cover and layout, we remain exceedingly grateful. Without them this book would not yet be a reality.

We also want to acknowledge Brian O'Connor, Ginny West Case and Martha Chamberlain for offering helpful editing suggestions.

And we offer thanks and appreciation to the dozens of individuals who participated in our classes, seminars, and workshops who convinced us that this material is important and life-changing.

Preface

Why Did We Write This Book?

The material in this book can help you make dramatic changes in your life. You can experience reconciled family relationships, restored marriages, and freedom from deep emotional wounds. Forgiveness and reconciliation can be realized with former spouses, parents, siblings, children and friends. Our prayer is that the material in the following pages will help you move through your journey toward the freedom that comes from forgiving and being forgiven.

Dr. William Carpenter

Dr. Ann O. Slimp

The Banquet

I glanced at my watch as the taxi circled the block where my appointment was scheduled. I was arriving a few minutes early. The invitation to a banquet in an unfamiliar part of the city had piqued my interest, and now the driver was having a difficult time finding the street address. Unfortunately, I wasn't much help.

I asked the cabbie to stop in front of the only building on that side of the boulevard. After I paid the fare and exited the back seat, I looked up at a large red brick structure that resembled an old gymnasium. Gray city-soot blanketed the windows located high above the sidewalk.

In the late afternoon sun, I made my way down the sidewalk and reached a flight of stone steps at the corner of the building. The first step was quite high, and it was worn from many years of use, a deep impression from so many steps before mine.

Who built this? I wondered.

Glancing around to see if this was the right entrance, I saw the red taillights of the taxi growing smaller in the distance. A little anxious, I climbed the steps to a set of large oak doors.

I tugged on an old brass handle and the door swung open to reveal a narrow hallway. Stonewalls on each side rose into the darkness above, and I marveled at the sight of a high ceiling, barely illuminated by a single band of light. Leaving the daylight of the boulevard behind, I stepped down from the entryway and stumbled into the hallway. As my eyes grew accustom to the near-darkness, I could see a long, narrow passageway stretching before me. I considered how strange this all seemed.

Someone sure made this difficult, I thought.

Moving cautiously, I glanced again at my watch but could barely see my wrist in the darkness. I paused for a moment – there in the hallway – and considered retracing my footsteps and leaving this place.

This must be the wrong address, I considered.

I again noticed the sliver of light that shot up to the ceiling. It came from the far end of the dark corridor. Remembering the taillights of the taxi and the empty street, I continued slowly down the narrow passage. The floor was rough cobblestone, and each footstep echoed off the walls surrounding me. I stepped gingerly; afraid I would trip on the uneven floor.

That's all I need. Fall down, tear my suit, and fail to continue this journey. Then a question occurred to me. *Am I really on a journey?*

I kept moving forward at a snail's pace, feeling my way down the wall and pausing now and then to reflect on my little adventure. I pondered what awaited me where the light shown through. Finally reaching the end of the hallway after so many doubts, I stood facing another set of doors. That so much light could shine through such a narrow seam surprised me. The light illuminated yet another step at my feet. Leading up this time, the step was barely deep enough to support my foot. I leaned forward just enough to push on the doors and felt resistance. Apparently, the doors were badly warped, stuck in their frame from the bending and twisting that comes with age.

Or was someone pushing from the other side?

Although it was difficult to keep my feet on the narrow step, I gave the doors a good shove and forced them open. *At last*, I breathed aloud and peered around into a large gallery.

The room was very large, much larger than what I would have expected from the appearance of the building from the street. Centered in the hall, a long table draped in white linens was surrounded by simple wooden chairs. Large platters, napkins, place settings, and silverware adorned the table rather informally. Nothing looked lavish or expensive. In fact, the simplicity caused me to wonder if I had overdressed for the occasion. It was then that I caught the wonderful aroma of grilled meat and fresh spices. Reassured that I had, indeed, found my destination, I moved confidently into the silent room.

No one greeted me. The air was mysteriously still. I glanced at my watch. It was still early. I decided to browse. The sound of my leather heals against the aged hardwood floors echoed through the hall. There was no artificial light. Only the late afternoon sunlight strained through soot-coated windows near the top of the brick walls.

Walking beside the table, I saw at each place setting a card leaning against an empty wineglass. Surprisingly, the first card I read had my name printed in a simple but clear style, affirming again that I had found the right place. It was strange that I should be the first to arrive and stranger still that the first card I happen to read was my very own, but the anxieties I had experienced earlier began to subside. Glancing at the place setting next to mine, I read the name of a man who had once been my employer. My heart sank. Years before, I had considered him lacking integrity. A master manipulator, he had lied and deceived all those around him – including his own family. This man had hid behind the guise of a caring person in order to win people's trust. I was annoyed that he was also a guest and bristled at his placement next to me. For a moment, I considered moving his card.

Then I glanced at the other place setting next to mine and read with relief the name of my wife, again written in the same simple and clear style. I expected her name to be there. We had both received an invitation and made previous plans to meet here.

Wondering if I might know any other guests, I circled around the table, not recognizing any of the dozens of names I happened across. Then I came to a card that caused me to flinch with a sudden and somber pain: the name of my ex-wife. So many dark memories washed over me. I remembered her saying she no longer wanted to be married to me. I remembered her saying that she had been planning the split for quite some time. And I remembered her failing to tell me about the other man. I strongly resented seeing her name.

I don't think I want to be here, I thought with a great discomfort. *I should leave now.*

I took a few determined steps toward the doorway and long corridor, every bit aware of the journey I had made to get here. Then I hesitated. My wife would soon arrive, and I needed to warn her of this potentially uncomfortable situation. Pausing there in the center of the hall, my anger began to subside. It slowly gave way to reason. I wondered who else was invited, and I continued to circle the table.

At the place setting located directly across from mine, I glanced down to see a card with five letters printed on it: N-A-N-N-Y. I smiled a smile of blissful joy as a strong sense of warmth and love enveloped me.

"My dear grandmother," I whispered aloud, breaking the silence surrounding me. That whisper, and the feeling of warmth that accompanied it, seemed to last a lifetime. But then a tremor of realization shook me from deep within my soul.

"Nanny's been dead for years."

Looking up, I realized for the first time that this table – indeed the entire hall – appeared to be endless. Both stretched as far as I could see – and far beyond! In my sudden surprise, I began to walk faster along side the endless length of the table. As far as I could tell, each place setting was the same; each had a name card leaning against an empty wine glass. Then I broke into a jog. None of the names were familiar to me. A little confused, I opened into a full run. At this speed, the names were a blur, but I could still read them. They were the names of strangers. In fact, many of the names I couldn't pronounce.

At that moment, I understood the hall was not an ordinary hall, and this table was not an ordinary table. Out of breath, I came to a stop, hands on knees and breathing heavily. Although I still could not see the far end of the table, I knew who sat at the head of it. Could it really be Jesus, the Lamb of God? Was this the long-promised biblical wedding banquet that would never end? Could this be the feast of the Kingdom – the eschatological banquet? I would not want to miss this banquet for anything! And I was here!

Excited and a little overwhelmed, I realized the name of every person I had ever known was here, somewhere around this immense table. Catching my breath, I glanced around wondering: *Will they all show up? How many will ignore their invitations? How many will decide that this address is the wrong address, that this is the wrong banquet hall, as I had nearly done? How many souls will venture only a few feet down the dimly lit corridor before turning back? And I wondered, Will anyone be turned away?*

I felt embarrassment and regret. My earlier thoughts about moving my former employer's name card were entirely inappropriate. This was not *my* banquet. I had not created the invitation list, and I certainly had not sent out the invitations. I knew nothing of the seating arrangements. I could never risk forfeiting the opportunity to see my grandmother again or fail to sit with my wife forever because of my arrogance, pride, and discomfort. *Who would allow their petty grudges and anger to keep them from such a place as this?* Yes, there were those who I had planned to never see again, much less sit next to them – forever! Yet, I would not miss this banquet for anything in the world.

Then I wept for a moment and felt very immature. I realized in my weeping that a long-promised reunion was about to take place, and I did not want to miss it.

Glancing at my watch, I realized there was still time. I ran to the doors, down the length of the dark hallway, and up the steps to where the doors led outside. Tugging the doors open, I bounded down the stone steps into the street and dim daylight, all the while thinking, *I must find my wife.* I had to make sure that she found the banquet. Once I had accomplished that, I would rush to invite as many people as I could – to let them know that they also had an invitation and a place at the table waiting for them. The only reason any seat would go empty is if someone chose not to be there. A panic overcame me.

Some might have thrown their invitations away. Others might have lost or misplaced them.

As I marched up the sidewalk, I saw a middle-aged couple quarreling across the street. I deeply wanted them to stop. I wanted them to forgive each other. More than anything else, I wanted them to know about their invitations. I wanted them to know that their names – along with so many others – are also on the table. They needed to see their foolish and petty arguing for what it was. I wanted them to know about this banquet. I wanted everyone to know. I did not want anyone to miss it – and certainly not forever.

The traveler in the banquet story received an invitation, made plans to travel alone to the destination, and upon arrival began questioning the path: "Is it worth the effort?" "Maybe I should turn around." Seeking forgiveness requires us to travel alone into risky territory. Seeking forgiveness means putting ourselves out there – at times allowing ourselves to be vulnerable. We must choose to embark on the journey – an intentional route with a distinct address – a haven of peace and a place of the reconciled.

Introduction

Forgiveness has become a popular topic in recent years. Major foundations have spent millions funding research. Newspapers and magazines have featured articles on it. Bookstores stock dozens of books on forgiveness, both secular and religious. Television and radio shows host people in real conflict for our entertainment, but few portray an attempt at authentic forgiveness.

Forgiveness is the doorway through which we can enter a life of health and peace – both for the forgiven and the forgiver. It is a sacred process, not to be used for entertainment, but honored and pursued, as a divine path to freedom.

In our ministry with individuals and churches, we have discovered that people are confused about what forgiveness is and is not. Forgiving is not excusing or forgetting the offense. Many people willingly forgive any manner of offense including the trivial and unintentional: the careless store clerk who short-changes them; the bad driver who inconveniences them, the neighbor whose pet disturbs their sleep. These experiences annoy and frustrate, but they are not the types of emotional or spiritual injuries that are addressed in this book.

The power of true forgiveness is best realized when you forgive someone whom you know: an irresponsible friend, an unfaithful spouse, an abusive parent, a rebellious child, an untrustworthy minister, or even the God who failed to meet your expectations. It is these types of injuries and wounds that this book addresses.

We believe our approach to forgiveness incorporates the truth of the Bible and the evidence of science, integrating biblical theology and current psychological research. In many models of forgiveness, God is not a part of the formula. We believe God embodies the forgiveness process. John Patton, a distinguished professor of pastoral care, has argued that, "Human forgiveness is impossible without the presence and working of God."[1] Along with Patton and others, we are convinced that forgiveness is impossible without God. Forgiveness is a spiritual and miraculous healing process.

11

The Many Layers of Forgiveness

In this book we propose a diagram that illustrates the entire spectrum of forgiveness. To experience *complete* forgiveness one must not only forgive others but also ask for forgiveness, forgive oneself, and deal with anger one may feel toward God. We illustrate this "picture" of forgiveness with four circles that are interwoven. Each circle represents a different part of the forgiveness process including: 1) seeking forgiveness; 2) forgiving self; 3) forgiving others; and 4) resolving issues with God following a loss.

These issues of forgiveness overlap. The center of the diagram depicts *guilt*. Guilt is a common experience for those who struggle with forgiveness, and it will be addressed in further detail throughout the book.

By exploring these issues, we will guide you the reader through various paths of forgiveness. As you embrace this process, we hope you will experience the freedom that results from offering and receiving forgiveness.

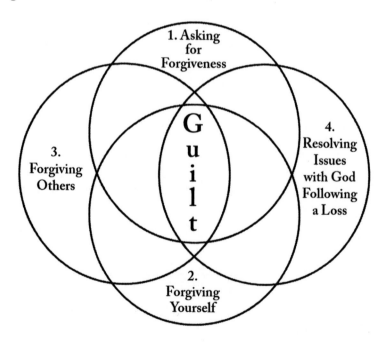

The Circles of Forgiveness

Each circle in the diagram of forgiveness illustrates an important piece of the entire picture of forgiveness:

1) *Asking for forgiveness*

2) *Forgiving yourself*

3) *Forgiving others*

4) *Resolving issues with God*

Circle One: Asking for Forgiveness from God and Others

Seeking forgiveness from others requires willingness to acknowledge your mistakes and when possible, ask for forgiveness from the one whom you have hurt. Circle One explores the biblical model for requesting forgiveness and provides suggestions about how, when, and from whom you might choose to seek forgiveness, as well as information about keeping yourself safe in the process.

Circle Two: Forgiving Yourself

When you acknowledge that despite your flaws, you are forgivable, you begin forgiving yourself. Accepting that you are forgivable can be difficult. Many struggle with shame – the belief and feeling that they are unworthy of affirmation, love or forgiveness. Self-forgiveness will be discussed in this section.

Circle Three: Forgiving Others

Section Three will describe the five steps in the process of forgiving people who have hurt you. You will find biblical and psychological principles that will help you move towards health and freedom while you learn to forgive others.

Circle Four: Resolving Issues with God Following a Loss

People often experience confusion and anger in response to a significant loss or an unexplained tragedy. It is easy to feel abandoned, neglected, and punished by God. This section examines this experience, discusses the process of speaking one's anger to God, and explores forgiveness from God.

A Note Before You Begin

It is impossible for us to write a book that addresses every person's specific circumstance. Just as there are many ways of arriving at a geographical destination, so there are different routes to achieve forgiveness. We offer this book as a map. Use it along with your own prayerful considerations to determine the best route for your journey to forgiveness. Trust God and your intuition and your mentors about when and how you will embark on this journey.

Before you begin, we offer three suggestions: 1) Tell a pastor, friend or counselor about your commitment to become more forgiving. Ask for support during this process. 2) Start a forgiveness journal in which you can respond to the suggested written exercises, and 3) Be prepared to experience some uncomfortable emotions such as sadness or anger. Feelings are a normal part of working through forgiveness. Remember – you are not alone. The God who is the source of all grace and forgiveness is with you.[2]

You must decide if you are going to be overcome with anger or resentment. You will make the choice to act destructively or to act to resolve the conflict and reconcile your relationships. One path leads to inevitable destruction. The other path leads to freedom, peace, and joy. The choice is yours. May God bless you as you journey into the miracle of forgiveness.

We begin the journey of forgiveness by hearing or receiving an invitation, just as the traveler did in the banquet story. It may be received in a dream, heard through the words of an inspiring speaker, spoken by our inner voice, or experienced through subtle nudges of the Holy Spirit. Our journey begins when we respond to the invitation to forgive or be forgiven.

What Does the Bible Say About Forgiveness?

"Forgive us our debts, as we forgive our debtors," Jesus taught his disciples to pray. Even now, hundreds of millions of people say these words every week, some every day. Yet, this is an unforgiving world filled with people who intentionally cause harm. People lie to one another; they cheat, steal and betray each other. People do these things - strangely enough - not to their enemies, but to those to whom they are closest. To understand what forgiveness is, it is necessary to gain a biblical understanding of what Jesus was praying in his words "forgive us our debts..." The exploration begins in the Old Testament.

Forgiveness in the Old Testament

Forgiveness is first formally depicted in the Old Testament as an act that God gives to those who pray and offer up sacrifices. The Mosaic Law provided specific ways through which a sinful Hebrew could approach God and seek forgiveness through rituals and prayers.[3]

To seek forgiveness from God, a man abiding by Hebrew law was expected to be sincerely sorry (Psalm 51:7). He was also expected to offer a sacrifice of livestock or crops for the priests to burn as an offering to God. This ritual was intended to refresh sinners and allow each to begin anew to seek God's will. God expressly desired these acts of contrition and forgave those who were honestly remorseful, who confessed, and offered sacrifice. In short, the Mosaic Law laid down instructions about what a sinful person must do in order to be forgiven by God.

In addition, portions of the law known as the *Lex Taliones* specifically defined sins that injured others and God. Such laws also provided instruction about how a person could make restitution for sins they had committed.

Although the Old Testament is filled with images of forgiveness as an act of grace that God offers to repentant people, we also see examples of people forgiving other people. In Genesis 25:19 - 33:12, we are told the story of Jacob stealing the blessing and birthright, which rightly belongs to his older brother Esau. Initially, Esau vows to kill his brother.

However, years later Jacob returns home and sends gifts to his brother before his arrival. Jacob experiences God's grace in the open arms of his brother as Esau smiles and welcomes Jacob home. Anyone who has been truly forgiven can relate to Jacob as he says to his brother, *truly to see your face is to see the face of God* (Gen. 33:10).

Also, the story of Joseph and his older brothers who sold him into slavery illustrates the human capacity for forgiveness. Joseph's rise to power in Egypt and his confrontation and eventual forgiveness of his brothers can encourage you on your journey of forgiveness. Joseph was able to see God's saving hand in his misfortune, and he told his brothers, *Even though you intended to do harm to me, God intended it for good ...* (Gen. 50:20). These two Old Testament stories bear witness to the miracle of forgiveness between the offended and the offender.

To understand forgiveness fully, you must also understand the concept of atonement as described in the writings of the Old Testament. Today, atonement is understood to mean "to make amends" or "to repay or make satisfactory an injury or loss."[4] Ancient Mosaic Law spelled out the observance of an annual Day of Atonement, *Yom Kippur*, in the sixteenth chapter of Leviticus. During this observance, Hebrew's were expected to pray and practice self-denial. In addition, their sins were symbolically placed on a goat and sent away. This "scapegoat" was literally driven away from the community and into the wilderness, bearing the sins of the people.

Forgiveness in the New Testament

The use of the scapegoat was an integral part of living in a restored relationship with God in the Old Testament. As the New Testament unfolded, Jesus assumed this role for all people. Jesus, the Messiah, revealed the desires of the Creator in a new and complete way. His death and resurrection were defining statements of the sacrifice that God made for the sins of the whole world. They established holy atonement with God the Father. As the author of Hebrews writes:

> He entered once for all into the Holy Place, not with the blood
> of goats and calves, but with his own blood, thus obtaining
> eternal redemption. For if the blood of goats and bulls, with the

sprinkling of the ashes of a heifer, sanctifies those who have been defiled so that their flesh is purified, how much more will the blood of Christ, who through the eternal Spirit offered himself without blemish to God, purify our conscience from dead works to worship the living God (Heb. 9:12)!

Jesus' act of love serves as the ultimate sacrifice so that all those chosen and adopted by God can begin a restored relationship with God. The Christians of the New Testament must have understood in a very real way that they were *bought* with the price of Jesus' blood.

Jesus' words and actions in the Gospels testify to the importance of forgiveness. Jesus communicates the importance of forgiveness in the "Parable of the Unforgiving Servant" (Matthew 18:23-35). In this parable, two servants are depicted who owed sums of money. The first servant owed the greater amount - 10,000 talents. One talent was the equivalent of more than 15 years' wages for a laborer. Ten thousand was the largest number in their economic system. It was an unimaginable amount of money. The second servant owed much less, about the equivalent of a hundred days' wages. Consider the lesson Jesus taught:

For this reason the kingdom of heaven may be compared to a king who wished to settle accounts with his slaves. When he began the reckoning, one who owed him ten thousand talents was brought to him; and, as he could not pay, his lord ordered him to be sold, together with his wife and children and all his possessions, and payment to be made. So the slave fell on his knees before him, saying, "Have patience with me, and I will pay you everything." And out of pity for him, the lord of that slave released him and forgave him the debt. But the same slave, as he went out, came upon one of his fellow slaves who owed him a hundred denarii; and seizing him by the throat, he said, "Pay what you owe." Then his fellow slave fell down and pleaded with him, "Have patience with me, and I will pay you." But he refused; then he went and threw him into prison until he could pay the debt.

When his fellow slaves saw what had happened, they were greatly distressed, and they went and reported to their lord all that had taken place. Then his lord summoned him and said to him, "You wicked slave! I forgave you all that debt because you pleaded with me. Should you not have had mercy on your fellow slave as I had mercy on you?" And in anger his lord handed him over to be tortured until he would pay his entire debt. So my heavenly Father will also do to every one of you, if you do not forgive your brother or sister from your heart (Matt. 18:23-35).

The magnanimity of the king in this parable is incredible. The king knew this servant could not possibly repay such a debt - even in a thousand lifetimes. This servant fell down and pleaded for mercy from the king and promised to repay the debt. All those in attendance at that scene had to know that the servant's promise could never be fulfilled. But the king forgave his servant this huge debt.

Jesus challenges you to forgive those who *owe you*, just as God forgives you. He equates sinning with owing a financial debt to God or owing your neighbor. This debt can never be repaid. Jesus' teaching equates forgiving with releasing a person from debt. This premise not only is central in the ancient Hebrew laws, but also is essential in the New Testament understanding of forgiveness. When you forgive, you relinquish the expectation that the offender will ever be able to *pay you back - to make restitution.*

Choosing to let go of your expectation that someone will repay you is also an essential piece of forgiveness.[5] This concept will be explored, forgiveness being synonymous with releasing the offender from debt, throughout the remainder of this book. The structure of this book follows the progression in Jesus' parable: You must realize, like the first

20

servant, that God loves, forgives and accepts you. Then, you must be forgiving of others.

Forgiveness is Releasing the Debtor from Debt

As the Christian faith evolved in history, the message of repentance and forgiveness continued to develop. The Apostle Peter proclaims in the Book of Acts,

> *Repent, and be baptized every one of you in the name of Jesus Christ so that your sins may be forgiven; and you will receive the gift of the Holy Spirit (Acts 2:38).*

Paul used the word *justified* in his writings to communicate the idea of salvation and forgiveness. This legal term was used in ancient courts to describe a person who had paid the full penalty for his crime and was restored back to his place in society. Because Christ paid the price for our sin, we are *justified* in Christ.

> *For there is no distinction, since all have sinned and fall short of the glory of God; they are now justified by his grace as a gift, through the redemption that is in Christ Jesus, whom God put forward as a sacrifice of atonement by his blood, effective through faith" (Romans 3:22b-23).*

The idea that debt was incurred when a sin was committed not only was prevalent in ancient cultures, but also is reflected in our language today. Think of the expressions you use to describe someone who has wronged you. You may say things like "I'll make her pay" or "He really owes me." When someone hurts you, you likely feel in your gut that he or she *owes* you something. So how can that broken trust be repaid? How can anyone restore one's life after years of childhood abuse? How does he or she compensate for betraying marriage vows? Such debts simply cannot be repaid.

By the same token, you cannot repay the debts you owe God, created by your own sinful acts. What you can do is accept the gift of God's forgiveness available through Jesus' sacrifice. You can also choose to forgive and, in doing so, live Christ's message and imitate His life. In choosing to forgive, you are faithful to Jesus' message and are freed from the bondage of resentment and the desire for repayment that can never be satisfied.

Forgiveness is freedom. Forgiveness is the canceling of a debt. Forgiveness is surrendering your justifiable right to hurt someone back. Forgiveness is the balm that cleanses emotional wounds and heals them. Once relinquished, the offense no longer affects the offended. Does this sound impossible? Humanly, it is. But

Forgiveness is a miracle born out of the grace of God and made perfect through Jesus.

forgiveness is a miracle born out of the grace of God and made perfect through Jesus. You are invited to explore that miracle of forgiveness for yourself.

Study Guide

What Does the Bible Say About Forgiveness?

- Identify some of the rituals for forgiveness and atonement spelled out in the Old Testament. Do any of these rituals or practices make good sense to you? Can you see how Jesus being the "Lamb of God [dying for the sins of the world]" takes on significant meaning for Jews that became the first Christians? How so?

- Consider financial indebtedness as a metaphor for forgiveness. Does "The Lord's Prayer" take on a new meaning for you when you offer the phrase, "Forgive us our debts, as we forgive our debtors?" Do you prefer to say, "Forgive us our trespasses," or "Forgive us our debts"? What difference does it make to you?

- Re-read Jesus' parable in Matthew 18:23-35. Can you identify with the first servant and allow God to be in the role of the king? Can you think of a person you have not forgiven and identify him or her with the second servant? Does the parable make intimate sense to you now? In what way(s)?

We accept an invitation, however we receive it, to begin the journey to forgiveness. The journey may take you down long winding paths, through unchartered forests, or through dark corridors, but know that God is with you and that your courageous decision to journey forward will bless both you and others. The journey may stimulate old fears, chronic fears that may have been dormant for years. Realize that you have been carrying a burden, however unwittingly or innocently. To many, wearing a formal business suit is a burden, and at times can be a hiding place.

How Does Shame Interfere
with Forgiveness?

It is our belief that shame interferes with one's ability to forgive. Many people confuse shame with guilt, which further interferes with forgiveness. Exploring shame and guilt will help us clarify and understand the distinction.

Differences Between Shame and Guilt

In developmental psychology, Erik Erikson's classic theory of human growth teaches that shame issues develop earlier in life than those related to guilt.[6] In the Bible, humankind doesn't even make it out of the Garden of Eden before shame emerges. Guilt is the feeling you have done something wrong. Shame is feeling that you *are* something wrong.

What Is Shame?

Shame is a fear or sense that something is terribly broken inside us. Carl Schneider offers a clear and concise definition: "[Shame] is a painful experience of the disintegration of one's world. A break occurs in the self's relationship with itself ... The self is no longer whole but divided. It feels less than it wants to be ..."[7] Those who struggle with shame fear that others can detect this internal brokenness. Shame-filled people feel inferior, inadequate and unacceptable.[8] Shame can be a painful experience, so painful in fact, that many people engage in strategies to hide from or defend against it.[9]

Shame-filled people often defend themselves in a number of psychological, spiritual or behavioral ways. For example, they may repress or deny their shameful feelings. People of faith who struggle with shame may hide behind their "righteous indignation" or spend a lot of time placing blame on others.[10] Shame-filled people may engage in other hiding behaviors that develop into destructive patterns such as drinking too much, spending too much, or attempting to be too perfect.

What Is The Human Origin Of Shame?

Most psychologists agree that the messages you receive in your formative years largely form how you view yourself. The ways your parents, grandparents, teachers, and other significant people interact with you influence your self-perception. Essentially families teach children how to develop relationships with self and others, how to maintain healthy boundaries, and how to trust. If families are not stable enough, children can develop shameful feelings about themselves and accept mistaken beliefs about who they are.

Heinz Kohut's theory of human development helps one understand shame further. He proposed that a child who does not receive an appropriate amount of nurturing and boundary-setting could experience a disconnection with his or her self, parents and others. This lack of a healthy balance between nurture and appropriate boundaries can often result in shame, or the experience of feeling unacceptable to others and to oneself.[11]

As depicted in the illustration below, shame can cloud your perspective on everything, including forgiveness. When you are frantically trying to defend against shame, you cannot fully engage in forgiving or being forgiven.

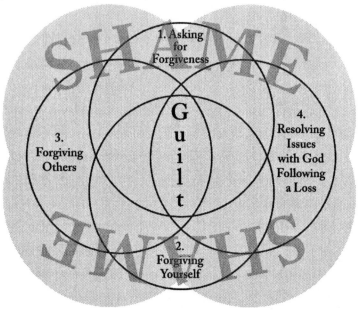

The Essence Of Shame: The Lie

Essentially, all shame-based feelings are the result of human error. Shame comes from either mistaken messages that you have received from significant others, or lies that you have adopted as the truth. Martin Buber identified the lie as the soul committing "...specific treason against itself."[12]

As previously mentioned, shame often results from inadequate nurturing or negative messages received during childhood. As the child grows, these messages are internalized and often amplified. Parents and other caregivers can often shame their children by relating to them as less than human - as objects to be controlled through fear and intimidation.[13] Repetitive comments like, "Are you stupid?" or "You are bad," may help to build a shamed-based identity in a child.

All people feel ashamed to some degree. But a shame-*filled* person allows shame-based thoughts, feelings, and behaviors to dominate their being. They feel virtually unlovable and find it impossible to do the work required to forgive (or be forgiven) until shame is healed. Thus shame interferes with forgiveness.

What Is The Biblical Origin Of Shame?

The story of Adam and Eve in the third chapter of Genesis helps to identify the root of shame. Adam and Eve lived together in paradise. All of their needs were met in grand proportion. They had dominion over all of creation and they had an intimate relationship with the Creator. There was one rule in the garden. This rule had been established for the humans' own good. God told Adam *not* to eat from the Tree of the Knowledge of Good and Evil. Adam and Eve were also, however, created with free will. They were free to make choices. They could choose names for the plants and animals. They could choose what to eat and they could choose what not eat. And they could choose to obey God or not to obey God.

The story reveals that Eve encountered a serpent that enticed her into considering eating the fruit from the Forbidden Tree. The serpent challenged Eve by asking a question, *Did God really say, 'You must not eat from any tree in the garden?'* (Gen. 3:1) In a subtle and sinister way, the serpent enticed Adam and Eve to question God's design of them and the garden. The serpent continued with *You will not die . . .* and tempted her with a false promise that she would essentially know what God knew if she ate the fruit (Gen. 3:4). Then Adam ate the prohibited fruit, too. *Then the eyes of both were opened, and they knew that they were naked; and they sewed fig leaves together and made loincloths for themselves* (Gen. 3:7).

When God called to Adam and Eve asking, "Where are you?"(Genesis 3:9), they were hiding in an attempt to disguise their shame. Adam responded to God's question by confessing that he was afraid and was hiding because he was naked. God knew that His one rule had been broken and asked, *Who told you that you were naked? Have you eaten from the tree of which I commanded you not to eat?* (Gen. 3:11). Adam and Eve then attempted to defend against their shame by blaming others. God exacted the promised consequences for this betrayal, first on the serpent and then on the man and the woman.

Harmony in creation had now been disrupted. Paradise had been tarnished. Trust had been exchanged for lies and deceit. Honest communication had been

The preoccupation with self and a desire to hide and protect oneself becomes a theme of destructive sinful patterns for generations to come.

replaced by deception and blaming. As Walter Brueggemann states in his commentary on Genesis, "the humans are suddenly becoming preoccupied with self. '*I* was afraid.' '*I* was naked.' '*I* hid.' '*I* ate.'"[14] This preoccupation with self and a desire to hide and protect oneself is revealed as a theme for destructive sinful patterns for generations to come.

For purposes of this exploration, shame is defined as *the acceptance of the lie that one is unlovable or not of value.* The pain of shame is an unnamed ache or emptiness from not being nurtured and affirmed adequately. Shame is the human response to the lie against creation and the Creator. That lie essentially says, *God is wrong. You are not loved. You are not of value.*

Shame results from human failure, both in Adam and Eve's case and in today's human relationships. You may have accepted the messages that you are so flawed that you are unlovable. These messages are distortions of God's truth - the truth that you are God's child, infinitely valued and loved, redeemed through Christ's resurrection. Once you realize that truth, and can claim it, *the truth will set you free* (John 8:32).

But, like Adam and Eve, if you accept the lies, you likely attempt to cover up. You want to run from the pain of shame. You do not want your nakedness - your imperfections - to be exposed. The Hebrew word for naked, *arun*, is usually used to describe somebody stripped of protective clothing and naked in the sense of being without defenses.[15]

People today do not use fig leaves to defend against shame as Adam and Eve did. The culture of today is much more sophisticated. You might use alcohol or drugs to numb the pain. You may spend money and seek power to feel in control. You might search for fault in others in order to distract yourself from your own sense of brokenness, and to manipulate others to look away.[16] You may disguise your fear with "righteous indignation," thereby refusing to see *the log in your own eye* (Matt 7:3). These are the preferred hiding places of modern day culture.

After Adam and Eve's failure, God responded with grace (Gen 3:21). Most people do not know that the texture of fig leaves is very rough. In their desperate attempt to hide, Adam and Eve covered their nakedness and shame with leaves that are similar to sandpaper. They were living in the pain that was sewn together by their own hands. In the biblical story God removed the leaves and gave Adam and Eve "garments of skin" (Genesis 3:21). It is a gentle scene, where God's love and grace made them more comfortable with themselves. God clothed them. God did for them what they could not do for themselves. They could not deal with their shame. But God could, can, and does with Grace.

In the Bible, to be clothed is to be given life.[17] But Adam and Eve could not clothe themselves. They could not clothe each other. Their clothing, like the Garden of Paradise and all of Creation, was a gift from God.

Remember, in the beginning of the story the man and woman were naked and they felt no shame. Scripture essentially tells us we will all be naked - exposed before God. *And before him no creature is hidden, but all are naked and laid bare to the eyes of the one to whom we must render an account* (Hebrews 4:13). But, here is the good news: God clothes us in righteousness, dressing us in white linens, even those washed in the blood of the Lamb (See Revelation 7: 9-14).

God's message to you, specifically in the teachings of Jesus, is that God loves you with your uniqueness and your imperfections. God loves you with a love so large that Jesus was sent to serve as your sacrificial lamb. If you accept any message about yourself other than the gift of God in Christ, you accept a lie. Ironically, it is this trust – faith in the redemptive power of Christ that enables and empowers you to begin the process that heals shame.

God's Healing Response To Shame: God-Worth

The process of healing shame begins with trust. You must learn to trust God and develop trust in at least one safe human relationship. God's message to all is a message of acceptance. The challenge is to accept God's gift of love without feeling as though you have to deserve it.

In order to become whole, you must seek to heal from your shame. Lewis Smedes says, "We are responsible for what we do with what other people did to us."[18] When it comes right down to it, adults who struggle with shame suffer because they have allowed childhood shaming experiences to continue to control their adult relationships. This is why they usually need outside help, divine and human, to resolve their shame.

Shame-filled individuals need a sense that God knows them, accepts them, and will never let them go. However, this free and unmerited gift from God is difficult to accept for some individuals.[19] Acknowledging and accepting God's grace is the beginning of healing shame.

In prayerful reflection, you can find messages of worth and acceptance. Also, engaging in trusting relationships, first with Jesus Christ and then with safe people, will foster your sense of true worth. In addition, you need to invest in a genuine community of faith or church family that will encourage your true sense of value. Smedes writes, "If you wonder where God's grace can be found, find yourself a friend who is not afraid to hold you accountable. A friend who wants you to be as good a person as you can be, a friend who dares to confront your flaws . . . then accepts the whole of you in grace."[20]

In the creation story of Genesis, God declares everything as "good."[21] In so doing, God demonstrates the value placed on each creation. God also proves that you are valued through the witness of the patriarchs, monarchs, and prophets.[22] God offers humankind continual chances to be reconciled with their Creator (Isaiah 61:1-3). The ultimate illustration of this love is the hand-delivered message of acceptance, love, and grace given to all people in Jesus Christ (John 3:16-20). Therefore, *God-worth* is the concept that we, the authors, use to describe the most basic principle of being loved and valued by God. *God-worth*, in contrast to the concept of "self-worth" assumes that your intrinsic value comes from the redemption of Christ.

Shame is not overcome through status, money, power or attempting perfectionism. Shame is healed through the restoration of our relationship with God. You overcome shame when you accept the truth of God's grace and integrate that truth into your life. Truly, you are God's child and God's message to you is one of worth and value. Ultimately God-worth is communicated most vividly in the life of Jesus. Jesus said, *Do not be afraid, little flock, for it is your Father's good pleasure to give you the kingdom* (Luke 12:32).

When we allow *God-Worth* to be in and around us, we become better equipped to love others; thereby making forgiveness possible. The illustration on the following page depicts this concept of God-Worth, replacing the lie of shame.

> God-worth, in contrast to the concept of "self-worth," assumes that your intrinsic value comes from the redemption of Christ.

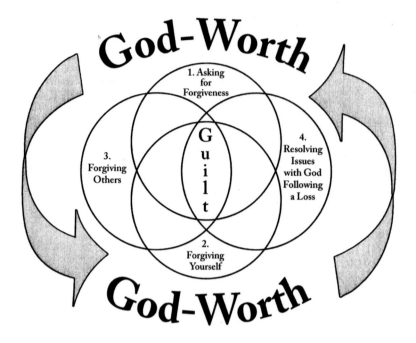

You cannot earn God's love. It is a gift. You cannot lose this gift - God's value of you. Paul said, "*For I am convinced that neither death, nor life, nor angels, nor rulers, nor things present, nor things to come, nor powers, nor height, nor depth, nor anything else in all creation, will be able to separate us from the love of God in Christ Jesus our Lord*" (Romans 8: 38-39).

In conclusion, we share with you a prayer that can serve as a reminder of who you are as a child of God's.

A Litany of a Person

image of God
born of God's breath
vessel of divine love
after His likeness
dwelling of God
capacity for the infinite
eternally known
chosen of God
home of infinite Majesty
abiding in the Son
called from eternity
life in the Lord
temple of the Holy Spirit
branch of Christ
receptacle of the Most High
wellspring of Living Water
heir of the kingdom
the glory of God
abode of the Trinity.
God sings this litany
eternally in his Word.
This is who you are.

-Abbey of Gethsemani

Study Guide

How Does Shame Interfere With Forgiveness?

After reading about the concept of *God-worth,* read the activities below and select one or more to awaken your spirit to the truth that God values you:

1. Identify some of the lies you have accepted about yourself. List them briefly on paper, or share them with a trusted friend. Pray for them to be lifted. Replace those lies with one or more images from the following:

   a. Read Zephaniah 3:17-20, and consider how you might be a *delight* to God. God treasures you. List in your journal or on a sheet of paper two or three ways that God delights in you. Identify ways in which you are a unique treasure of God's. What gifts has God given you? What skills have you developed that God 'exalts'? If you have difficulty doing this, imagine how your best friend would respond to the above questions about you.

   b. Read Psalm 103, and then list all of the positive things that are said about you in each of these verses. Consider how you are the Sovereign Lord's possession.

2. Draw a horizontal line across a page of paper. The beginning of the line represents your birth. Write your birth date at the beginning point of the line. The end of the line is your death. Divide the line into five to ten year equal segments, depending on your age. Then, place at least one "X" on the page (in each segment that is possible) that represents a person in your life that made you feel valued or appreciated. Place a star (*) next to the "X" if you remember a particular comment or

experience that was pleasant. Now, pray and give thanks to God for all those individuals and experiences that blessed your life.

3. Draw two oval mirrors. Draw one as a distorted curved mirror similar to those at a carnival. Draw the other as a normal mirror. Draw a picture of yourself with all your flaws in the distorted mirror (or use words to describe yourself). Now in the normal mirror, draw how God views you (or use words to describe how God views you). Try to view yourself through the forgiving lens of God. Pray that you will glimpse yourself through God's loving eyes. Say to yourself "God loves me and I have worth."

4. Thank God in prayer for God's love and acceptance of you.

During most journeys of any distance there are times we find ourselves in darkness. On the journey of forgiveness the corridors of the soul seem dark and foreboding at times. But then we glance at the wall directly beside us and notice a faint shadow. We realize that where there is a shadow there is a light. And that realization brings us comfort. As we continue on the path toward forgiveness, the light grows ever brighter.

Circle One:
How Do I Seek Forgiveness?

How Do I Ask For Forgiveness?

Throughout this forgiveness process, you may become aware of your own mistakes. You might wonder, how can I ask for forgiveness? The following is written to respond to this question.

Guilt is what you usually experience when you do something wrong. It is the nagging awareness of remorseful anxiety, that heaviness that follows an act that violates your own sense of right and wrong. Authentic guilt can often lead to an honest self-evaluation, which ultimately can lead to more sincere relationships with God and others.

Guilt, in contrast to shame, occurs in most people when they have acted in a way that is not consistent with what they think is right. As you

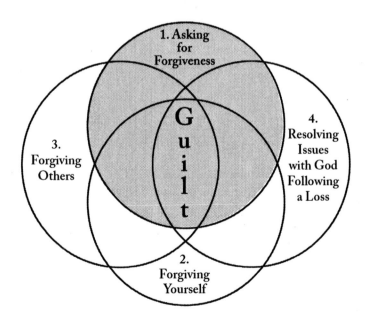

may recall, shame is the feeling of internal brokenness, a sense that you *are* something wrong. Guilt is the feeling that comes after you have done something wrong. It is important to distinguish between shame and guilt in order to be equipped to ask for forgiveness in a genuine way.

How Do I Remedy My Guilt?

Paul writes to the Corinthians: *Now I rejoice, not because you were grieved, but because your grief led to repentance; for you felt a godly grief, so that you were not harmed in any way by us. For godly grief produces a repentance that leads to salvation and brings no regret, but worldly grief produces death* (II Cor. 7:9-10).

According to Paul, when you are able to accept your wrongdoing and honestly repent, you are able to remedy your guilt. To repent means to turn or to change direction. When you repent or change and seek forgiveness, the weight of guilt is lifted from you. You shed your guilt "as filthy garments" and your life is more open to God's grace.

However, guilt can be a tricky and unpleasant emotion. Some people often spend great amounts of energy trying to avoid guilt. Others are so steeped in exaggerated guilt and shame that they often feel false remorse for actions and events over which they have no control. Understanding how you cope with guilt can better equip you to realize true forgiveness.

When you repent or change and seek forgiveness, the weight of guilt is lifted from you. You shed your guilt "as filthy garments" and your life is more open to God's grace.

How Do I Avoid Guilt?

Some people avoid guilt by ignoring the harm they have done or by blaming the victim of their wrongdoing. It is easier to slip into the self-deception that "he deserved it" rather than feel the weight of your mistakes. An entire entertainment genre has developed around publicly blaming others and verbally or physically threatening those who have committed wrongdoings. The idea seems to be, if you can put on a loud and threatening show then you need not feel guilty for any wrongs you have committed.

Others justify wrongful acts by claiming that it was for a "greater good." Such a person argues that the "ends justify the means," regardless of the harm done in the process. Many wars and criminal acts have been justified in this manner. Often people, particularly those in authority positions, have an overblown sense of entitlement and feel that rules of conduct do not apply to them, thus making guilt and apologies unnecessary. This has been tragically evident over the past several decades among some public figures, such as politicians and clergy.

Others equate feeling guilty or saying "I'm sorry" with weakness. They cannot face their guilt, own up to their mistakes and apologize, because they fear being vulnerable. They fear that saying "I'm sorry" may make them powerless in some way, when actually the ability to take responsibility for one's actions is a sign of character strength.

Accepting responsibility for your mistakes is not popular. The cultural norm clearly leans toward avoiding accountability and responsibility. Have you bought into the cultural norm of avoiding responsibility? Do you avoid saying "I'm sorry?" Do you deny or minimize your errors because you expect yourself to be perfect? Admitting mistakes and acknowledging guilt requires humility.[23] Those who cannot or will not acknowledge their errors will find it difficult to ask for forgiveness. If you find yourself avoiding guilt and accountability, engage in some unflinchingly honest self-evaluation. You will then be better prepared to move on in the journey of forgiveness.

Do I Harbor False And Unmerited Guilt?

In contrast to those who avoid guilt, others feel guilty constantly. People who feel compelled to frequently apologize about the slightest error or inconvenience are troubled by the *sorrow of the world* as Paul describes (II Cor. 7:9-10). These people feel responsible for circumstances beyond their control and are most likely not only struggling with feelings of false guilt, but are also struggling with unresolved shame. They feel guilt, not for what they have done, but for who they are.

This can be true for over-achievers or people who appear perfect.

People who appear to have it "all together" can be struggling to camouflage their guilt and shame by their achievements. Such achievements can be fragile disguises for false guilt. It is another way to hide shame.

Do you over-commit yourself? Do you struggle with constant feelings of guilt? If so, re-examine the source of your guilt. Do what is necessary to heal the shamed part of you. Then you will be better equipped to proceed with forgiveness.

How Do I Ask For Forgiveness From God And How Do I Ask For Forgiveness From Others?

In order to ask for forgiveness, you must be willing to engage in courageous self-examination. Viewing your flaws and humbly seeking forgiveness requires effort. But, in doing so you will be rewarded with freedom.

Scriptures reveal a process and order for asking for forgiveness. This process is very personal, but provides a universal model for seeking forgiveness from God and others. This model includes three biblical principles.

1. Confession
2. Repentance
3. Reconciliation

Biblical Traditions Of Seeking Forgiveness

In the ancient world when someone caused harm, the victim or his family would often seek unlimited retribution. A person seeking revenge might take drastic, often violent action. However, with the emergence of the *Lex Taliones*, the idea of limited retribution for a wrong suffered became the cultural and religious norm.[24] This was not only true for injuries between people, but also applied to violation of God's law.

The Law of the Levites was imposed on ancient Jewish life.[25] These laws dictated many aspects of daily activity, including religious and non-religious activities. For example, dietary laws dictated what a person could and could not eat. Other laws related to rules about borrowing and lending. When one of these laws was broken, there were ways that a Jewish believer could be cleansed and make amends to God and the community. For example, offering sacrifices of livestock was a common practice for attaining atonement for the Jewish cultures of that period. There were, in fact, specific guilt offerings that Jewish believers could present at the Tabernacle - or, later in history, the Temple - in order to cleanse themselves from guilt. These offerings provided a ritual that gave structure and meaning to the process of making amends to God. Chapters 4-7 and 13-14 of Leviticus include many rituals for atonement - absolving guilt and returning to a right relationship with God.

The New Testament offered different perspectives on forgiveness and emphasized the call to and need for repentance. The historical Christian church instituted a variety of rituals to equip individuals to deal with and resolve guilt-related issues.

Post-Biblical Traditions Of Seeking Forgiveness

As cultures have developed, so have rituals in Jewish and Christian traditions that provide methods for seeking and receiving forgiveness. Rituals are important. They give structure and meaning to significant moments. Rituals also help to mark the moments of forgiveness from God and others. A few common rituals are listed below:

- The Roman Catholic Sacrament of Reconciliation (formerly known as Penance): This process includes confessing one's wrong doings to a priest, completing some acts of penance - various forms of prayer, retreat, good works, or other activities, accepting absolution and being reconciled with God and the community.

- The Benedictine practice: After giving instruction from the Bible, the leaders ask each worshiper to identify issues that require forgiveness. Worshipers then submerge their hands in a large bowl of water, "holding" the grievance in their cupped hands. As they pray for the grace to forgive, gradually their hands open to symbolically 'release' the grievance."[26]

- The Lord's Supper or Holy Communion: This ritual calls for confessing one's sins with sincere remorse, symbolically laying those sins upon the altar, repenting and taking on the body and blood of Christ, mindful of the sacrifice offered to experience and proclaim God's grace.

- Jewish High Holy Day of Atonement: These Ten Days of Repentance includes Rosh ha-Shana and continues to the end of Yom Kippur. The purpose of these days is to allow for the atonement of sins against God - not against persons. (There must be an act of penance to the person one injured for forgiveness to take place between humans).[27]

- In the Orthodox tradition, the Sunday before the beginning of Lent is called Forgiveness Sunday. The community gathers for a vespers service, in which each member prostrates him or herself before other members, and asks forgiveness for acts that might have hurt or offended the other person. They declare to each other, "If anything I have said or done has hurt or offended you, I ask forgiveness." After forgiving each other, they share the kiss of peace.

These rituals are all founded on and illustrate the three biblical principles mentioned earlier: *Confession, Repentance and Reconciliation.*

It is frequently said that God's forgiveness is unconditional. However, although God's grace is offered unconditionally, grace and forgiveness are not identical. Forgiveness emanates from God's grace, but numerous examples in the Bible demonstrate that there are conditions for being forgiven. The first of these conditional principles is confession.

Principles Of Seeking Forgiveness

Confession

Identifying your transgressions and honestly confessing those errors is the first step in seeking forgiveness. Confession requires you to be courageously truthful about your wrongdoing. Confessing means you agree with God that your attitudes, your words, or your actions have been wrong.

When you confess, you specifically express that you were wrong. Confession also implies a sincere desire to change.[28] Until you actively confess your specific wrongdoing to God, you cannot fully seek divine forgiveness.[29] In addition, confessing your wrong doing to the person whom you injured, if

Forgiveness emanates from God's grace, but numerous examples in the Bible demonstrate that there are conditions for being forgiven. The first of these conditional principles is confession.

that person is safe and available, is the beginning of seeking forgiveness from him or her. The biblical mandate on confession is consistently clear.[30]

If we confess our sins, he who is faithful and just will forgive us our sins and cleanse us from all unrighteousness (I John 1:9).

Your first confession should always be to God (I John 1:9). God has promised to forgive you and cleanse you if you confess your sins. You should also confess your sins to someone else - a spiritual friend, a community to whom you are accountable, a minister or Christian counselor (James 5:16).

In many situations you may need to confess face-to-face to the person you have injured (Matthew 5:23-34).[31] When doing so, use wisdom in your confession. Be sensitive to the words you choose. Be aware of your motivation for confession. For example, your confessions should be honest but not laced with hurtful details. Seek counsel if necessary to clarify your motives and method of confession. Maxie Dunham tells us that confession and self-examination go together as one discipline.[32]

Confession *invites* restoration of the relationship.[33] Confession requires you to demonstrate humility and remorse, and invites the person to whom you confess to begin forgiving you. Confession means relinquishing your pride and standing vulnerable in the sight of the one you injured - God and the victim. One author suggested that a person who has abused a child should demonstrate humility and sorrow by kneeling in front of the child and the other members of the family, confessing and asking for forgiveness.[34] Many people often take this posture when offering prayers to God, yet seldom if ever are willing to demonstrate such humility in front of people they have wronged. What a powerful statement this would make if more people were able to do so.

Some question the necessity of confession between people of faith. Dietrich Bonhoeffer, a martyred Christian theologian, proposed that those churches that do not encourage confession and repentance dispense "cheap grace":

> *Costly grace is the treasure hidden in the field; for the sake of it a man will gladly go and sell all that he has. It is the pearl of great price . . . it is the call of Jesus Christ. Such grace is costly because it calls us to follow . . . Jesus Christ. It is costly because it costs a man his life, and it is grace because it gives a man the only true life . . . Above all, it is costly because it cost God the life of his Son. . . .[35]*

The biblical instruction is clear, confession is essential in seeking forgiveness from God and from others.

In Psalm 51, as David is confessing his sin, he calls out to God for inward change. This prayer-filled Psalm not only illustrates a sacred model for how to confess to God, but also shows how to honestly express a desire to change (Psalm 51:2, 6, 10):

> *Wash me thoroughly from my iniquity, and cleanse me from my sin. For I know my transgressions, and my sin is ever before me. Against you, you alone, have I sinned, and done what is*

evil in your sight, so that you are justified in your sentence and blameless when you pass judgment. Indeed, I was born guilty, a sinner when my mother conceived me. Create in me a clean heart, O God, and put a new and right spirit within me.

This honest desire to change is the path that leads to the second step in seeking forgiveness – repentance.

Repentance

The second necessary component in seeking forgiveness from God and others is repentance. The classic understanding of repentance is "to turn" or "to change directions." We translate the English word *repent* from several different biblical words including the Hebrew *nacham* (denoting a change in mind or heart) and *shub* (meaning to turn away from evil and towards God). Also, *metanoeo*, a Greek word that is traditionally translated as "a remorse and a change in thinking" appears in the New Testament 66 times. When you repent, you resolve to change, and demonstrate your penitence.

Theologically, then, to repent is to change one's mind and heart, and this

To repent is to change one's mind and heart, and this results in turning away from sin and turning toward or back toward God.

results in turning away from sin and turning toward or back toward God. Scriptures offer numerous examples of God's expectation for repentance in both the Old and New Testaments:[36]

If my people who are called by my name humble themselves, pray, seek my face, and turn from their wicked ways, then I will hear from heaven, and will forgive their sin... (II Chronicles 7:14).

I will tell you there will be more joy in heaven over one sinner who repents than over ninety-nine righteous persons who need no repentance (Luke 15:7).

The Biblical mandate is clear. Once you are aware of your wrongdoing and humbly confess it, you must change. Acknowledging your mistakes by confessing them is simply not enough. You are to change direction and get a new heart. You must identify the origin of your transgression, be it a personal flaw or limitation, and set about the process of changing it.[37] Repentance refers to a genuine change of heart and mind that is necessary for a real change of behavior to take place.

Change, however, is hard. To deliberately change is one of the most challenging activities humans can undertake. Ask anyone who has tried to stop smoking, overeating or using an addictive substance. Anyone who has learned to alter unhealthy interpersonal patterns such as poor communication, explosive anger, or passive-aggressive patterns, knows that change can be very difficult.

Change requires honest evaluation, revelation, courage, and a desire to move forward in your relationship with God and with others. Change often requires diligent effort over a period of weeks, months and sometimes years. Often it is too difficult a task to do alone. Seek wise counsel and support from loved ones, clergy or a competent Christian therapist to help you in your process of change.

Not only does change require courage and determination, it is most important for you to rely on God's grace.[38] As you are attempting to change, you may find yourself weighted down by the memories of your transgressions. You may find yourself wallowing in guilt. Perpetual guilt has nothing to do with genuine forgiveness. Once you have confessed and begun to change direction, you must shift your eyes from your failings to God's grace. Letting yourself become paralyzed by guilt or shame is synonymous with buying the lie that Christ's sacrifice was not enough. Peter, one of the founders of the Christian tradition, illustrated true remorse and repentance.

Then Peter remembered what Jesus had said: "Before the cock

46

crows, you will deny me three times." And he went out and wept
bitterly (Matt 26:75).

Yet, Peter did not allow this failure to paralyze him. Rather, he became one of the most significant leaders in the early church displaying immense faith in the face of persecution. John the Baptist said, *Bear fruit worthy of repentance* (Matthew 3:8). This is the mark of true repentance. It is evidenced by a changed life - new and different commitments and attitudes that others can witness. Changed behaviors and expressions can be witnessed by others and lead to the possibility of reconciliation.

Reconciliation

In addition to confession and repentance, scripture offers a third step on the path to forgiveness from God and others - that of reconciliation. There are various meanings in scripture related to the term reconciliation. In relationship with God, reconciliation means to have your transgressions forgotten or not remembered. That is, once you confess, repent and seek reconciliation with God, it is as though your sins never existed. God's forgiveness is that complete.

Reconciliation is restoration of a relationship. This harmony may take many different forms, and can mean different things for different people. Reconciliation for some can mean a fully restored relationship. For others, to be reconciled may simply mean moving beyond anger and resolving not to harbor resentment about a transgressor, while having no actual relationship. The Bible offers a number of passages that emphasize the importance of reconciliation.[39] The Gospel of Mark provides us with a clear example from the words of Jesus:

> *So when you are offering your gift at the altar, if you remember*
> *that your brother or sister has something against you, leave your*
> *gift there before the altar and go; first be reconciled to your brother*
> *or sister, and then come and offer your gift* (Matt 5:23-24).

Remember, biblical teachers and writers used many economic terms to describe forgiveness. Reconciliation is such a term. Today you "reconcile" your bank statements. Often people think of "investing" spiritually, emotionally, and physically in relationships. You invest your time, your energy, sometimes your money and possessions. You invest in your dreams and you invest your trust. Wounds often leave you feeling as though someone owes you or that you owe someone else. God's grace, experienced through the process of forgiveness, allows these spiritual accounts to be audited and balanced by Jesus' sacrifice.

Again, the mandate from scripture is clear. You are not only to be reconciled with God but also with your sisters and brothers. Being reconciled with God is illustrated most clearly in the Parable of the Prodigal Son.

The Parable Of The Prodigal Son

Then Jesus said, "There was a man who had two sons. The younger of them said to his father, 'Father, give me the share of the property that will belong to me.' So he divided his property between them. A few days later the younger son gathered all he had and traveled to a distant country, and there he squandered his property in dissolute living. When he had spent everything, a severe famine took place throughout that country, and he began to be in need. So he went and hired himself out to one of the citizens of that country, who sent him to his fields to feed the pigs. He would gladly have filled himself with the pods that the pigs were eating; and no one gave him anything. But when he came to himself he said, 'How many of my father's hired hands have bread enough and to spare, but here I am dying of hunger! I will get up and go to my father, and I will say to him, "Father, I have sinned against heaven and before you; I am no longer worthy to be called your son; treat me like one of your hired hands."' So he set off and went to his father. But while he was still far off, his father saw him and was filled with compassion; he ran and put his arms around him and kissed him. Then the son said to him, 'Father, I have sinned against heaven and before you; I am no longer worthy to be called your son.' But the father said to his slaves, 'Quickly, bring out a robe – the best one – and put it on him; put a ring on his finger and sandals on his feet. And get the

fatted calf and kill it, and let us eat and celebrate; for this son
of mine was dead and is alive again; he was lost and is found!'
And they began to celebrate (Luke 15:11-24).

In the parable, the youngest son asked for the equivalent of his future inheritance. The parable does not reveal whether the father recognized the son's impulsiveness. All we know is the father gave his son the money for which he asked. The image of the father illustrates how God allows us free will, even if our desires are born out of recklessness, pride or ingratitude.

When the son is confronted with his poverty, he comes to his senses. Only in his most desperate hour, when he was physically and spiritually starving, did he honestly see himself for who he was. He realized how he had sinned against Heaven and against his father. He was filled with humility, felt guilt, and began to hold himself accountable.

The father, we are told, felt *compassion* for his son. So happy was the father to have the son home that he could not wait for the boy to reach the house. Instead, he ran to him and threw his arms around him. He celebrated his return and demonstrated his joy by throwing a lavish party. His forgiveness was truly complete. God, like the father in the parable, awaits your humble confession and repentance and reconciles with you.[40]

The Compassion Of God

The parable of the Prodigal Son provides a model for asking for forgiveness from God and others. The story also teaches us much about God's compassionate character and his desire for us to be reconciled. Scriptures reveal God's compassion.[41] Isaiah 49 illustrates an example of a biblical statement about God's compassion: *Can a woman forget her nursing child, or show no compassion for the child of her womb? Even these may forget, yet I will not forget you* (Isaiah 49:15).

We also see God's compassion revealed in the character of Jesus:

> *When he saw the crowds, he had compassion for them, because*
> *they were harassed and helpless, like sheep without a shepherd*
> (Matt 9:36).

49

The *compassion of God* is not only clearly expressed and demonstrated in the ancient scriptures, but becomes personified in the person of Christ as well. During his years of ministry, we find that Jesus demonstrated his compassion through acts of kindness such as feeding the five thousand.

Mark 8:2 tells us that Jesus saw that the crowd was hungry, and he had "compassion on them." Jesus also reached out to individuals who had violated Levitical law and forgave them. He forgave a woman who was about to be stoned for committing adultery (John 8:3-11). Jesus also forgave a woman who was known as a sinner while he was dining in a Pharisee's house (Luke 7:36-50).

Jesus provides the ultimate sacrifice through which you can access God's forgiveness - his death and resurrection. When you observe Holy Communion (the Lord's Supper), you are reminded of Jesus' supreme sacrifice and his divine ability to restore your relationship with God. To borrow from the metaphors in the parable of the Prodigal Son, God - through the love of His Son - runs to you, wraps His arms around you, and welcomes you home.

Being reconciled involves the willingness of two parties: the wrongdoer as well as the one who was wronged.

Reconciling With Others

Being reconciled involves the willingness of two parties: the wrongdoer as well as the one who was wronged. As the wrongdoer, you have no control over the willingness of the victim to reconcile. You should ask for forgiveness and invite reconciliation but not coerce or pressure the injured person to reconcile.[42] You can, however, offer a complete apology by admitting your wrongdoing, demonstrating your desire to change, and asking the injured person for forgiveness.

What Is An Apology?

Many people have never witnessed, received or offered a complete apology. A complete apology includes three parts:

1) *Confession - naming the wrongdoing, admitting it was wrong and saying the words "I'm sorry."*

2) *Repentance - committing to not doing this act again.*

3) *Reconciliation - asking the question, "Will you forgive me?"*

For the mother who hits her child out of anger, a complete apology would sound something like this: "I am sorry. I was wrong to lose my temper and hit you simply because I was angry. I will not do it anymore. Will you forgive me?" By admitting your sorrow and confessing your wrongdoing, you demonstrate your willingness to hold yourself accountable. By specifically asking for forgiveness you communicate respect for the wounded person.

Also, when you apologize, refrain from offering a lengthy explanation or detailed reason why you did what you did. You may feel tempted to embed your apology within a long story describing the events that led up to your actions. But this only serves to muddle the apology. Offer an explanation only if the injured person asks for one.

Once an apology has been offered and forgiveness has been granted, then the process of reconciliation can begin. Reconciliation may not always mean restoring a relationship. For a battered woman who has protected herself (and possibly her children) by leaving; reuniting with the abuser would obviously put her at risk. For a husband whose wife was unfaithful, remarrying her without requiring her to demonstrate authentic change would be unwise. Restoration is only possible when the wrongdoer is repentant and seeks God's help in reconciling with those who have been hurt.

Face-to-face reconciliation may not be possible. The injured person may not be available due to distance, death, illness, or passage of time. You may find that facing the injured person would be physically or emotionally dangerous. In these instances it is important to consider how you might express your confession, repentance and desire to reconcile in a symbolic way. Read and complete the writing exercises in the following study guide.

Study Guide

How Do I Ask For Forgiveness?

Seeking Forgiveness From Others

1. Read the verse below. Meditate on this verse and consider how it might apply as you confess to God actions for which you are seeking forgiveness.

> *Hear a just cause, O Lord; attend to my cry; give ear to my prayer from lips free of deceit. From you let my vindication come; let your eyes see the right* (Psalm 17:1, 2).

2. Answer the following questions. Write your responses in your forgiveness journal.

    a. For what do I need to be forgiven?

    b. What morals or rules did I violate?

    c. How did my actions or words hurt another person? Who?

    d. How did these actions or words hurt my relationship with God?

Working Toward Repentance:

1. Read Isaiah 55:6-13. Write a few sentences about how repentance is described in these verses.

2. Complete the following questions regarding your character:

   a. What character traits may have led to my actions that hurt others?

   b. Do I struggle with fully accepting responsibility?

   c. Might I be too prideful? Might I fear intimacy? Might I use substances, money, food or any habit to excess? How might these patterns hurt others?

3. Consider what you need to do to repent or "change direction" in your life. The questions below will help you begin a plan to change:

   a. Think honestly about the people with whom you spend most of your time. Are they helping to guide you in the direction you need to go? What relationships might you need to let go or change?

   b. How do you spend most of your time? Where do you work? How do you spend your leisure time? How much time do you spend with God?

   c. Where do you spend your money? What priorities do you consider important regarding your finances? Are your priorities reflected in your spending habits?

d. In what way do you need to renew your relationship with God?

Reconciliation

1. Read the Parable of the Prodigal Son and imagine yourself in the place of the younger son (Luke 15:11-31).

    a. Tell God what you have done.

    b. Confess your wrongdoing.

    c. Tell God that you desire to repent and imagine God's response.

    d. Imagine God celebrating your return.

    e. Look in God's eyes and see His immeasurable love and complete forgiveness.

2. Follow the steps below with the person from whom you would like to seek forgiveness:

    a. Consider the person from whom you need to seek forgiveness. If need be, ask God to show you whom you have hurt. With whom do you need to attempt reconciliation?

    b. Write down what you have done, without excuses or explanation. Challenge yourself to focus on your actions and refrain from including the circumstances that "made you do it."

    c. Write the words "I was wrong." Write the words "Will you forgive me?" Read your apology and imagine yourself saying these words to the one from whom you wish to seek forgiveness. This activity may take some practice.

d. You are almost ready to offer the apology. Before doing so, however, imagine how the injured person might react. He or she may express rage, mistrust, reluctance or apathy. Try to prepare for any possible reaction. Forgiving can take time, especially if the wound was deep and long lasting. Don't expect immediate forgiveness.

e. Consider when and where you might offer this apology.

f. Don't pressure or coerce the wounded person to forgive you. Invite forgiveness and let the wounded person make the choice.

When we make a decision to accept an invitation to forgive, we, like the traveler in the banquet story, must step into an unfamiliar and unsettling location and must leave the familiar arena of our lives. When we do so, we realize we weren't that comfortable after all. Although this process takes much effort, we know that this is a time to put away childish things and begin to mature and gain insight. We climb the first steps, begin to forgive ourselves, and move away from our self-imposed burdens - weight created by our own fears, denials and self-deceptions. We realize that even the longest journey begins with the first step.

Circle Two:
How Do I Forgive Myself?

How Do I Forgive Myself?

Self-forgiveness has been described as a process of confronting oneself, holding oneself responsible, confessing one's flaws, and transforming oneself.[43] In short, self-forgiveness can require some effort. However, the key to self-forgiveness is accepting the reality of God's grace.

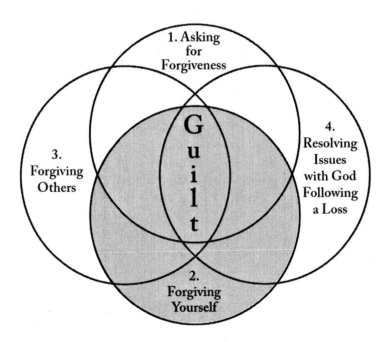

Forgiving yourself includes a process whereby you:

1) Accept that you have failed and acknowledge that you cannot fully repay the spiritual debt that you owe. Rely on the forgiveness and healing available through God's grace.

2) Embrace God's grace as a means of accepting yourself as imperfect but as a beloved child of God, always striving to become closer to what God would have you be. By accepting the reality of God's love and forgiveness, forgiving yourself becomes an act of letting go of shame and guilt, accepting some regret and living in the truth that God can and does forgive.

You may find it difficult to be compassionate with yourself. You may not want to look at the reality of your mistakes. However, it is important to remember that you can make no mistake that is larger than the love God has for you.

Christ calls for us to love God, love our neighbor and *love ourselves* (Mark 12:30*)*. Forgiveness is a characteristic of the love that God expects of us. Paul encourages us to *Clothe yourselves with compassion* (Col. 3:12).

Some might suggest that forgiving yourself is synonymous with casting off your responsibility. However, self-forgiveness requires you to embrace your responsibility, hold yourself accountable, repent and then move beyond the mistake. By forgiving yourself, you will confront your transgressions and open yourself to God's forgiveness and absolution.

Barriers To Self-Forgiveness

You may feel reluctant to forgive yourself. You may have unanswered doubts or questions that keep you from forgiving yourself. Questions are listed below that may have caused you to stop short of forgiving yourself:

• Do I really deserve to be forgiven? You may struggle with the idea of exchanging your shame for God's grace-filled view. The truth is that no one "deserves" forgiveness. If one relied on one's own goodness for forgiveness (of self and others), no one would be forgiven. Jesus' sacrifice and triumphant resurrection gives you the avenue through which you cannot only seek forgiveness from others and God, but also forgive yourself.

• What was my mistake? What led me to act in this way? You need to be unflinchingly honest with yourself. Consider any personality traits that may have contributed to the specific act that you now regret.[44] You often act of your own volition, but there are times that you may have allowed others to manipulate or control your behavior. As you uncover what may have lead to your specific behavior, you become better equipped to change these character traits.

• What do I need to confess to God? What do I need to confess to others? As discussed previously, confession is an essential step in asking for forgiveness from God and others. It is also essential in forgiving yourself. Obviously your confession should first be made to God, acknowledging your responsibility and repentance. Then, tell someone in your life about your mistake. Choose someone who will turn you toward God in a supportive and uplifting way. As Lewis Smedes wrote, "It takes a miracle of love to get rid of the unforgiving inquisitor lurking in the shadows of your heart."[45]

• Is restitution necessary? The *desire* to make restitution, though at times unrealistic, is at the heart of an honest confession. Even when you are aware that you do not have the power to restore what was lost, you may be left with the desire to demonstrate repentance in some concrete way. When forgiving yourself, a concrete act of restitution can help you mark the end of your self-torture and the beginning of your new self. Restitution is not necessary for self-forgiveness, but for some people it can be an important ritual. Throughout biblical history, rituals of guilt offering have been made as part of the process of experiencing forgiveness.

Restitution serves as a meaningful expression of your own desire to make a positive contribution (to a specific person or the world) in response to the harm you feel you have done. For example, a man who battered his wife will not be able to "make up" for his violent behavior. He could however, invest in a trust fund for his wife or children's future or donate to a charity that assists victims of domestic violence. It is up to you to decide whether you feel some form of restitution is necessary and what form that restitution should take.[46]

After you have identified the shortcomings that led to the transgression for which you want to forgive yourself, you need to choose to forgive yourself. First, you must acknowledge God's grace and the forgiveness made available through Christ. You learn most about God's compassion through the life of Jesus.

Jesus intentionally spent time with known sinners. He ate with them, befriended them and invited some into his inner circle. Jesus was criticized for eating with tax collectors and sinners (Mark 2:16). He invited Matthew, a tax collector, to be part of his disciples (Matt 9:9). He was criticized for healing on the Sabbath (Mark 3:4) and calling outcasts into God's kingdom (Mark 2:17). There was a good reason Jesus ministered to and befriended those who had failed in life - he loved them. Jesus loves you and reaches out through the cross to you, too.

The sinners in Jesus' time sought him out and constantly asked for compassion and healing. They accepted his message completely. You may on the other hand, hold back and refuse to accept divine forgiveness by holding yourself hostage, by not forgiving yourself. How presumptuous we are in not forgiving ourselves when our debt has already been paid.

After accepting the reality of God's forgiveness, it may be necessary to act in some concrete way in order to demonstrate self-forgiveness. The following is a list of possible examples with which you may choose to celebrate forgiveness:

- Write a parable of your own including the wrongs you have committed against God. What would you say? When your parable is complete, choose a place of worship (either traditional or personal) and take your parable with you. When you are alone, read the parable to God making it a prayer. Ask God to forgive you. Meditate on the parable of the Prodigal Son (Luke 15:11-24) and silently imagine God's response to you. Imagine the way God might welcome you home and celebrate your homecoming. Thank God for His forgiveness.

- Review your church's rituals for Holy Communion (The Lord's Supper). Deliberately examine the Scriptures and prayers that your church advocates when observing the Lord's Supper. Meditate on these prayers and then deliberately participate in a public observance of Holy Communion, asking for and celebrating forgiveness.

- Baptism - getting baptized or reenacting baptism, can serve to celebrate God's forgiveness. Some other cleansing ritual that you do alone (wash your hands, head, your body; plunge into a pool, river, or lake and emerge 'cleansed', etc.) could serve to mark forgiveness for you.

- Dedicate or rededicate your life before a community of faith at the altar/chancel rail of a church. This can serve as a dramatic profession of your desire to live a life in and for forgiveness.

- Write a prayer that celebrates the forgiveness you claim. Pray this prayer privately or in a small gathering of trusted believers.

- Pray the prayer below. It is a popular prayer of confession from a Holy Communion Worship Service (with personal pronouns substituted for the corporate pronouns).

> *Merciful God,*
> *[I] confess that [I] have not loved you with [my] whole heart.*
> *[I] have failed to be obedient. [I] have not done your will,*
> *[I] have broken your law, [I] have rebelled against your love,*
> *[I] have not loved [my] neighbors, And [I] have not heard the cry of the needy.*
> *Forgive [me,I] pray. Free [me] for joyful obedience,*
> *Through Jesus Christ [my] Lord. Amen.*[47]

Claiming Christ's Forgiveness

After participating in one or more self-forgiveness rituals, we encourage you to renew your thoughts about yourself and claim Christ's forgiveness as often as is necessary. We encourage you to use prayer and Scripture to help you keep your thoughts focused on your forgiveness. Some examples are listed below:

Read Psalm 32 and Psalm 130. Make these Psalms personal prayers and thank God for forgiveness.

Offer one of the following prayers or meditate on Merrill's words about forgiveness:

Gentle God, You call me your beloved, but sometimes I do not feel very loveable. Help me to forgive myself and learn to love myself as someone created in Your Image. Amen

Father, help me to remember that I am loved and forgiven. Amen. (Pause at three specific times each day and repeat this prayer three times.)

Great Mender of souls, we long to be loved, to be understood. Create in us the humility, strength, and courage to seek reconciliation, to heal the wounds of separation. Amen

Meditate on the following words about forgiveness by N. C. Merrill:

Blessed are those who know the grace of forgiveness, for their capacity to give and receive love is expanded, their souls are unbound, healed, and released to soar. Through forgiveness comes liberation, the freedom to receive God's grace, the desire to share and extend love. Seek then the One Who knows all hearts; ask forgiveness of all that separates you from love. Rejoice! For what was broken will be made whole! Give thanks to the Beloved, Who is merciful and kind![48]

Study Guide

How Do I Forgive Myself?

1. Read Psalm 32:1-7 and Psalm 51. These scriptures relate to King David's adulterous relationship with Bathsheba. How did David express his remorse? How was his faith expressed through the petitions of confession, repentance and lament? What does this scripture say about David's praise to the God of forgiveness?

2. Read Psalm 27. Then, pray the Psalm. Offer it as your own. Then, rewrite the Psalm as your prayer, asking God for clarity in dealing with the issues of blame in your forgiveness journey. Review your written prayer each day this week. Meditate on it and then re-write it and offer it to God.

3. Ask yourself the following questions and respond to them in your forgiveness journal:

   a. What did I specifically do that contributed to my injury or failure?

   b. Did I realize at the time I could be hurt by my own choices and behaviors? What prevented me from protecting myself?

   c. What will I need to do in order to forgive myself? What might I lose if I forgive myself? What will I gain in forgiving myself?

The journey to forgive others begins in the same way that any trip to a geographical destination begins – we seek a way to get there. The traveler in the banquet story kept searching for clues, looking for confirmation that the path he was following was the right one. While uncertain, the traveler proceeded down the dark corridor. The traveler had to let go of self-absorbed thoughts and force the door open. Are you ready to open the door to forgiveness?

Circle Three:
How Do I Forgive Others?

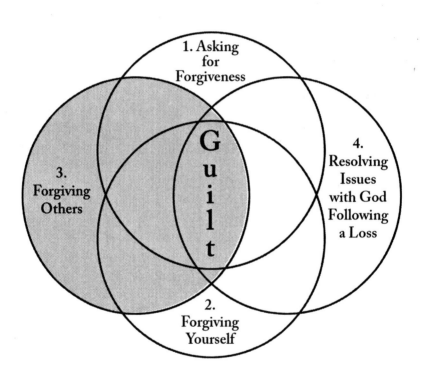

Am I Ready To Forgive Others?

Human beings can be unpredictable, clumsy, thoughtless and sometimes malicious. When people you trust violate that trust, you feel shocked. You feel hurt, angry, and sad. Having your trust seriously violated by someone you considered safe is traumatic. Usually the last thing you want to do is forgive. In fact you may want to think of ways to get revenge, to hurt your offender back. Forgive? Why should you?

Most Christians know that they are called to forgive through Scripture and the example of Jesus' life and teaching. However, the first impulse is to not forgive but to seek revenge. In learning to forgive, it is important to keep in mind what the author of Ecclesiastes said, *There is an appointed time for everything. And a time for every event under heaven* (Ecc. 3:1 NASB). Although you are called to forgive, you must recognize that there is an appropriate time to forgive.

Surviving The Injury

When you experience a serious physical wound, your body attempts to survive the trauma. In an attempt to maintain life, your body shunts blood to vital organs such as your heart and lungs. Once the immediate threat to your life has passed, and you receive adequate medical care, circulation usually returns to normal and your body begins to stabilize. In sum, when your life is in danger, your body first uses any means necessary to survive.

Similarly, when you experience a deep emotional wound, your body goes into emotional shock. Your emotional energy is focused on surviving the trauma and getting past the initial experience. Until the threat to your emotional survival has subsided, you are unable to develop plans or make good decisions. You will focus on survival. In short, you are in an emotional "survival mode."

When all of your energy is focused on simply getting past the initial shock of being betrayed, you need to do just that - survive the immediate disaster. If you find yourself struggling with depression or anxiety, or if your thoughts are consumed with revenge, you need to first recognize this as a "survival mode." This is the time to get support and to "rally the troops." Seek assistance from safe people in your life.

Call on trusted family members and friends for support. If you find yourself thinking about death or suicide, it is imperative that you find a competent counselor or admit yourself to the hospital.

When you are engaged in simply surviving an immediate crisis, you are not, nor should you be, concerned with the business of forgiveness. If you are in the "survival mode," then your main priority is to do just that – survive. The opportunity to forgive will come later.

Although it will take time, you can move beyond simply surviving and get your life back. Don't expect to get over it too quickly. Be gracious and compassionate with yourself. Take time to gather your resources before moving on.

Intense Emotions: Our Internal Alarm System

Many people have similar experiences when they face deep hurt. You may have thoughts of revenge or get overwhelmed with feelings of rage. This may surprise you and be inconsistent with who you think a Christian should be. However, such thoughts and feelings are to be expected. Although you may have the impulse to seek revenge, these wishes are often expressions of your anger. Anger is understandable. Revenge is not. Acknowledge that you are angry and choose not to act on thoughts of imagined revenge.

In addition to vengeful thoughts, you will likely have intense emotions: sadness may become depression; anger may become rage; and the desire for retaliation may become the impulse for revenge. This is to be expected for most people. We suggest that emotions are God-given and ask that you see them as what they are - signals that you have been violated. Intense emotions could be thought of as God's "alarm system" to let you know something is amiss. Don't ignore these signals. Embrace these feelings as part of your God-given alarm system. You will be better equipped to respond in a healthy and thoughtful way. You can choose to protect yourself from further injury. You can choose to seek support from friends and counselors.

The Special Circumstance Of Childhood Trauma

What if you were emotionally, physically, spiritually or sexually abused as a child? Countless children live in families where dysfunction wreaks havoc on their lives. Those who grow up with childhood wounds often take the consequences of their trauma with them into their adult years. If you are trying to understand and forgive injuries sustained during childhood, it is most important that you realize you were not to blame. Children are never responsible for actions of adults or older children. It is also essential that you find a qualified pastoral counselor or mental health professional who is experienced in assisting in childhood trauma.

When children sustain severe wounds, their lives are often thrown into chaos. They attempt to cope with this chaos with any means at their disposal. Patterns of dysfunction often emerge simply as means to survive the trauma. For example, a girl may become sexually promiscuous as a result of neglect or abuse at home. She may simply be searching for a genuine connection and confuse sex with intimacy. A boy who picks fights at school may be acting out what he sees his parents do at home. Such dysfunctional patterns may continue for years and need to be identified and addressed in a safe environment with a qualified counselor. You will be better equipped to forgive if you understand the trauma and its long-term effects. Therapy or pastoral counseling can help in this process.

Study Guide

Am I Ready To Forgive?
Assessing Readiness to Forgive Others

1. Read Ecclesiastes 3:1-8. What do these verses suggest regarding coping with difficulties that arise in life?

2. Read the following Psalms and write a brief description of the emotions the writer must have been experiencing at the time: Psalm 13, Psalm 40, Psalm 27, Psalm 32, Psalm 72, Psalm 92. In what ways might these Psalms reflect your emotional experience?

3. Are you ready to forgive others for the offenses they have perpetrated against you? If you feel you are not ready, consider what you need to do in order to get ready? What might you have to surrender if you forgive? What might you gain if you forgive?

The journey to forgive others challenges us to see ourselves as adventurers with a purpose – not as wanderers. Some settings remind us of how small we are and confuse us, just as the traveler in the banquet story. It is in these moments that we realize that what we seek may be much more accessible than we suspect.

Do I Have To Forgive?

You may wonder if you *have* to forgive the people who have hurt you. The truth is simple. Forgiveness is a choice - your choice. No one can force you to forgive. However, choosing to forgive has meaningful benefits while not forgiving can have negative consequences. By not forgiving, you may miss your opportunity to fully participate in God's banquet.

First, not forgiving can lead to hurdles in our relationship with God. Christians who know they have not forgiven struggle with guilt for not having followed the biblical mandate to do so. This can lead to distance from God. Jesus' words in Matthew 6:12,14 and 15 imply that God forgives according to the degree to which you forgive others:

> *And forgive us our debts, as we also have forgiven our debtors. And do not bring us to the time of trial, but rescue us from the evil one. For if you forgive others their trespasses, your heavenly Father will also forgive you; but if you do not forgive others, neither will your Father forgive your trespasses. (Matt 6:12-15)*

Second, remaining at odds with an offender leaves you forever spiritually and emotionally bound to him or her in an unhealthy alliance. When you refuse to forgive, you surrender a part of your life to the offender. You yield power to the offender. You allow the offense and the offender to control some part of you. You may say to yourself, "She does not deserve forgiveness." But, choosing not to forgive is to stay trapped in resentment and fear and may lead you into a life sentence of unresolved bitterness.

When you refuse to forgive, you surrender a part of your life to the offender.

Third, not forgiving often leads to unresolved blame and hostility, which can negatively affect your health.[49] More specifically, hostility has been correlated with heart disease, while unexpressed anger has been correlated with elevated blood pressure.[50] As you move through the forgiveness process, blame and hostility subside and you experience positive emotions. Research suggests that these positive emotions can actually boost your immune system.[51] Furthermore, forgiveness has also been linked with improved mental health.[52] This leads to the scientific speculation that forgiveness is indeed ultimately good for your health.

Choosing to forgive can help improve your relationships and give your health a boost. Choosing not to forgive can leave you at odds with God and others and have a negative impact on your health. So, learning to forgive is an essential step to physical, emotional and spiritual wholeness.

What Does It Mean To Forgive?

Many people struggle with forgiveness because they feel conflicted about seemingly letting the offender "off the hook." Therefore, it is important to remember that forgiveness is not the same as condoning the offense or excusing the offender's behavior. Forgiving does not require you to be reconciled with the offender. But, it can help you reconcile negative feelings you have about the offender. When you forgive, you take full stock of how you were hurt and choose to release the debt that the offender owes you. Forgiveness is not a feeling but a choice - a continual process of choosing to free yourself from the burden of anger and resentment.

> **Forgiveness is not a feeling but a choice - a continual process of choosing to free yourself from the burden of anger and resentment.**

Forgiveness is also a choice that requires some specific action on your part. When you forgive, you fully acknowledge the impact of the injury and choose to forgive despite the immensity of your wound. When you forgive, you free the person from the debt, and you free yourself. When you forgive, you stop waiting for the offender to make things right and relinquish your expectations that the debt will be paid.

Basic Assumptions

Before exploring the process of forgiving others, it is important to be aware of three assumptions that were made in building this model of forgiveness. First, it is assumed that you have been hurt in a serious way. Emotional hurts come in varying degrees. Emotional wounds of some magnitude - the "biggies" - leave you wounded and raw. Therefore, this model is a means to forgive those serious wounds.[53]

Second, it is assumed that the person you are learning to forgive is someone you know. Although strangers can and do hurt you, people in whom you trust are the ones to whom you are most vulnerable. Therefore, the majority of examples in this book describe injuries caused by family members, friends, and colleagues.

Finally, it is assumed that you have moved beyond the "survival mode" described earlier. Your emotions have become a bit more manageable and you are aware of the losses you sustained as a result of this emotional injury. You have begun to grieve over some of the associated loss and have a desire to forgive. That transition is a miracle of God's grace and love.

Why Should I Forgive?

Believers are called to forgive. Each time a person prays the Lord's Prayer, he or she asks God to forgive as he or she has forgiven. However, some actions seem beyond forgiveness. Those who commit the "run of the mill" sins seem rather easy to forgive, but not those who purposely set out to hurt you. You may wonder how God can expect you to forgive those who deliberately and deeply hurt you. What about people who prey on innocent children? You may think, *God will surely allow me to harbor some bitterness for those people.*

Injuries of great magnitude seem beyond forgiveness when people attempt to forgive others without God's help. However, you can choose to forgive because you are forgiven. Forgiveness is a gift that was offered by Jesus, and through the help of the Holy Spirit, you are empowered to forgive. By forgiving you throw off the burden of the injury and regain your hope.

Jesus taught the importance of forgiveness through his words and his example. His ability to transcend his own pain on the cross, asking

God the Father to forgive those who tortured him, is an overpowering testament. His message is clear when Peter asks, *"Lord, how many times shall I forgive my brother when he sins against me? Up to seven times?" Jesus answered, "I tell you, not seven times, but seventy times seven"* (Matthew 18:21-22).

Where Do I Begin?

This model of forgiveness requires you to explore a series of questions. Taking time to answer these questions for yourself will lead you on the path to forgiving those who hurt you:

Step One: How was I hurt? How do I feel about that hurt?

Step Two: Who is responsible for my injury? What do I feel the   offender owes me?

Step Three:Will my life ever be the same? How do I relinquish the role of victim?

Step Four: How will I release the offender from this debt?

Step Five: Who do I now become?

Study Guide

Do I Have To Forgive?

1. How would you have answered the following questions, if you had answered them before reading this section? What role does forgiveness play in the life of a Christian? Are there circumstances in which a Christian is "excused" from forgiving? How would you answer these questions now?

2. Do you think unforgiveness may interfere with your participation at the banquet described in the banquet story? How?

The traveler in the banquet story was surprised by some names at the banquet table. How could those people be invited? How is it possible that God expects us to forgive people who have hurt us with such deliberate malice? Acknowledging the hurt and relying on God's healing power is one of our first tasks in forgiving.

Step One:
How Was I Hurt?
How Do I Feel About That Hurt?

Once you have moved past the "survival mode" described previously, you are now ready to begin the process of forgiveness. The first step in forgiving someone who hurt you is recognizing your wound and acknowledging what happened to you. It is important to recall the injury and the losses that accompanied your emotional injury.

Looking into your own woundedness is not easy. This process can be quite disconcerting, especially if the injury occurred in childhood or was traumatic (or both). In the journey of forgiveness you are invited to become an investigator into your own life. Ask, "What are the specific damages I have experienced?" This is what you eventually will forgive.

As suggested in the introduction, journaling can facilitate the forgiveness process. You may want to record your thoughts and feelings in your journal or confide in a trusted confidant. The study guides at the end of each section include questions that will help you think and write about the event. Talking and writing about your injury can help contain some of the anger and hurt. *As these feelings emerge, remind yourself that feelings are part of the healing process and that the most intense of these feelings will eventually fade.* Although you may never be totally free of the feelings, as you open yourself to God you will feel less burdened by the hurt and more able to move beyond it.

Telling Your Story

In order to forgive, you first must acknowledge the various ways in which you were injured. Take the time to describe what happened to you in writing or in some other tangible manner. You may prefer to record your feelings on a cassette tape or depict your experience in a painting, poem or drawing. See the exercises in the study guide to help you write about what happened to you.

As you reflect on your injury, you may notice that your emotions are rather "raw" regarding the incident. If you are still coping with the worst of the emotional fallout, you will need more time before proceeding with forgiveness. You may discover that this specific wound reminds you of similar situations in the past. Spend all the time you need to identify what happened to you and how you feel about it. If necessary, engage a qualified therapist to help you tell your story.

After you have satisfactorily described your injury, read over what you have written. You may feel the need to cry, scream, pound a pillow or just sit quietly and absorb the enormity of what happened. Hold onto the fact that even the darkest moments will fade as you move through the healing process. These intense feelings will not last forever. Sadness and anger are part of recognizing the damage done, but the most intense of these emotions are temporary.

Hold onto the fact that even the darkest moments will fade as you move through the healing process.

Taking Inventory

As you consider the specific way in which you were hurt, it is also important to consider the collateral damage that you sustained as a result of the injury. Just as a pebble thrown into a still pond sends ripples across the water, so your injury probably affected different areas of your life. Consider the impact on different areas of your life by taking an inventory at this moment:

As a result of this event or injury:

- How has my relationship with God and other Christians been affected? How have my relationships within my church changed?

- How has this event changed my friendships? Professional relationships? Social gatherings?

- How has this injury affected my financial life? Have there been legal ramifications?

- How has my family been affected?
- How have I been affected emotionally?
- How has my physical health been affected?
- How has my spiritual journey been impacted?

As you identify the losses you have sustained, it is important to give yourself time to grieve. Grieving is important in the healing process. Although grieving is not necessarily part of the forgiveness process, it will equip you to move on with forgiveness.

Exploring your life may have changed the way you think about yourself. Moreover, this injury has likely caused some permanent changes in your life. The world and the people in it may seem a bit more unpredictable, a bit more frightening. The injury may have changed the way you relate to others. Despite these changes, it is important to remember that you are made up of more than the hurts you have sustained.

In sum, you may not only have been hurt, but you may have to grieve what you have lost. You may need to think of yourself in new ways. You may essentially need to redesign your life. You may need to fight the lie of shame and remind yourself that *God treasures you.* No amount of injury can separate you from God's love.

As you acknowledge the scope of your hurt, remember that you are God's treasure. Below are scriptures that will reaffirm your value. Consider what they tell you about how much God values you. Memorize them if necessary. Post them throughout your house and remember that you are a treasure to God:

> *For I am convinced that neither death nor life, neither angels nor demons, neither the present or the future, nor any powers, neither height nor depth, nor anything else in all creation, will be able to separate us from the love of God that is in Christ Jesus our Lord (Romans 8:38-39).*

> *Praise to the Lord, to God our Savior, who daily bears our burdens (Psalm 68:19 NIV).*

For you created my inmost being; you knit me together in my mother's womb. I praise you because I am fearfully and wonderfully made; your works are wonderful, I know that full well. My frame was not hidden from you when I was made in the secret place. When I was woven together in the depths of the earth, your eyes saw my unformed body (Psalm 139:13-16).

For God so loved the world that he gave his only begotten Son that whoever believes in him shall not perish but have eternal life. For God did not send his Son into the world to condemn the world, but to save the world through him (John 3:16-17).

Biblical Illustrations *(see related questions on pages 83-84)*

There are numerous biblical characters who were hurt and chose to forgive. The illustrations below and throughout these five steps, serve as a catalyst for you to reflect on your injury. Esau, Joseph and the father of the prodigal son are explored at length. Take the time to read and familiarize yourself with the sections of scripture identified with each of the three characters. See the questions provided in the study guide to further explore the experiences of these characters. By exploring the hurt and forgiveness of these individuals, you can learn from them and imagine what their thoughts and feelings may have been. This may assist you in processing your own feelings and forgiveness issues.

Step One For Esau: Read Genesis 25:1-35:29

Esau lost his birthright. He sold it to his younger brother Jacob for a bowl of chili because he was hungry one afternoon (Gen 25:27-34). Esau also lost the family blessing. Esau was entitled to this blessing as the eldest son. But under his mother Rebekah's prompting, Jacob disguised himself as Esau and tricked his nearly blind father Isaac into granting him the blessing. Esau returned from a hunting trip to discover the cherished family blessing had been stolen from him.

This event cost Esau his birthright. It cost him the family blessing. It also cost him his brother who fled the family to save his own life. Esau probably lost trust in his mother. His father, who had always favored him, chose to do nothing to restore the blessing for him. Esau felt frustrated and confused. He felt betrayed. He was hurt and very angry.

Step One For Joseph: Read Genesis 37:1-50:26

Joseph's brothers abandoned him. They sent him away in chains with strangers from another country and culture. Joseph felt alone - a slave among slave dealers. He was sold to Egyptians. The "splendid" coat that his father had given him had been ripped away. He was torn away from everyone and everything he had known. He did not know if he would ever see any of his family or his home again. He had no idea what tomorrow would bring. Joseph was fearful and confused. He had been rejected and was alone. Joseph felt powerless.

Step One For The Father Of The Prodigal Son: Read Luke 15:11-31

The prodigal son was gone. The son had rejected his father, his family and his community. He had rejected his father's name. It was as if the younger son had screamed at the father in every way possible "I reject your values. I reject your dreams for me. I reject your love for me. You are only an object, to enable me to get what I want. Give me the money. You do not matter to me. I don't want to be like you." That father must have been devestated. He had just given away half of his wealth and he had lost his youngest son.

Study Guide

Step One: How Was I Hurt? How Do I Feel About That Hurt?

1. Write several paragraphs in a journal describing what happened to you. Use the questions below to help frame your description: In what ways were you hurt? How old were you? Did you have any means of protecting yourself? How are you still affected by the wound? Emotionally? Physically? Spiritually? Financially? From whom or from where did you draw your strength?

2. Answer the following questions in your journal. Spend adequate time with each question. What did you lose as a result of the injury? (Note: Include tangible losses such as finances, relationships, and property. Also consider the intangible losses you may have experienced such as a loss of self-esteem, security, and dreams for the future.)

How has the injury affected your faith and relationship with God? How long do you expect the injury to last? Do you feel parts of your life have been altered forever? In what ways? (Note: Initially, we may feel that this injury will never end. Think about it! When do you realistically expect this injury to end or hope it will end?)

3. Draw a sketch or write a word list to describe yourself in four ways: Who were you before the injury? Who are you now? How does God see you now? How will God see you in the future?

4. Create a time line by drawing a horizontal line through the middle of a page of paper. Then, put vertical lines intersecting the horizontal line and label each section to represent a part of your life such as: childhood, adolescence, age 20-30, 30-40, 50-60, etc. If you are younger, label them in 5-year increments. Then identify significant life events. Write names next to the event signifying who was important during those times. Finally, circle those names or events in which God's love was revealed to you. (This activity will help you put this hurtful event in a relative perspective in relation to your entire life.)

Biblical Illustrations For Step One

Step One For Esau (Genesis 25:1 – 35:29)

1. When Esau realized that Jacob and Rebekah had deliberately planned to take his birthright and blessing, how do you think Esau felt?

2. What impact might this realization have had on Esau's relationship with his parents?

3. What tangible and intangible losses did Esau suffer? Describe the grief he must have experienced.

4. What impact might this experience have had on Esau's relationship with God?

5. How might Esau's experience be similar to or different from your own?

Step One For Joseph (Genesis 37:1 – 50:26)

1. As Joseph was taken farther and farther from his home, what might have been some of his feelings?

2. Joseph was first a favored son and then a slave. Surely he must have been shocked initially. He may have hoped his father would search for him and rescue him. How might your experiences of shock, disbelief and injustice be similar to Joseph's?

3. Have you spent time wishing for someone to rescue you?

4. How did Joseph's experience influence his relationship with God? How has your relationship with God been impacted in similar ways?

Step One For The Father Of The Prodigal Son (Luke 15:11-31)

1. Any good parent sacrifices time, money and effort for their children. How must the father have felt as he watched his son depart with half of his assets?

2. Have you ever been rejected by someone you loved, someone for whom you had made sacrifices?

3. How might your experience be parallel to the father's experience in this parable?

4. How might the father have maintained hope that someday his relationship with his youngest son would be restored?

5. How does this parable remind you of your own story?

The journey of forgiveness will challenge you to make sense of what you have been taught and learned about your faith. Identifying and empathizing with the one who hurt you may cause you to question your understanding of God. Just as the traveler did not initially recognize the holiness of the banquet and had thoughts of rearranging the name cards, we may also wonder what God is up to as we move through our journey of forgiveness.

Step Two:
Who Hurt Me And Why?

Assessing Accountability

Once you have clearly identified the scope of your injury, it is time to consider who hurt you and why. Assessing accountability helps you unravel who is responsible for your specific injuries. It helps you clarify who was at fault while also allowing you to begin to develop compassion for the wrongdoer. As you gain more distance from the event, you will develop a healthier perspective.

Guarding Against Perpetual Blame

Assessing accountability helps you clarify who hurt you and how his or her deed led to your wound. It is an important step on the path to forgiving. Clearly identifying the offender is important and can allow you to get in touch with your inner strength. However, it is important to keep in mind that it is a *temporary* step. All too often people get stuck at this step, due in large part to their anger and resentment. It is easy to remain in a blaming posture. This often brings a *sense* of power over the wrongdoer. Perpetually blaming the offender can give you a false sense that you are "putting him in his place," if only in your own mind.

However, blame is not power. In fact, staying stuck in perpetual blame only interferes with your well being and forgiveness. Do not allow *blame* to set up permanent residence in your soul. This will only serve to erode health and peace in your life. This may be particularly tricky for Christians who know they are "right" or standing on moral high ground. It can be tempting to remain stuck in righteous indignation and refuse to give up your "high ground." After all, if you forgive, how can you continue to think of yourself as a "better" Christian? It is not a contest. Being right is not the prize.

Our culture encourages blame. Popular media is rife with television and radio shows featuring people who dramatically blame others for the difficulty in their lives. Arguments and fistfights are advertised between the "victim" and the "offender" as entertainment. Whether genuine or fabricated, viewers often relish the explosive blame. These types of displays perpetuate the idea that blame and violence are the only way to cope with hurt. However, blame itself cures nothing. It should only be a temporary step forward to forgiving offenses.

Although holding the offender accountable is an important step, blame alone does not lead to healing. Incessant or indiscriminate blame can turn to hate. Anger, bitterness and rage can ruin life, for as Lewis Smedes says, "Hate can become the carcinoma of the soul."[54]

Who Is Accountable?

Do you know who is responsible for your injury? Have you carefully considered whom to hold accountable? For many readers the answer is obvious. The offender is the one that perpetrated the offense. Maybe he or she is a parent, child, sibling, spouse, former spouse, friend or colleague. Clearly the wrongdoer is either responsible or at least partially responsible for your pain.

However, in the early and sometimes indiscriminate stages of your pain you might want to blame everyone. One wound might trigger memories of past wounds caused by others. You may be uncertain who is responsible for what layers of pain. Emotions can often be so intense that it is difficult to get clarity on whom to hold accountable for what offense. Using your forgiveness journal or talking about accountability with a trusted friend or counselor may be helpful during this part of the process. Once you know who hurt you, you know who to forgive.

Am I Accountable?

You may find yourself wondering if you played a role in your own pain. If this is the case, it is important for you to distinguish between events that were beyond your control and those events in which you were responsible. It is important to distinguish between authentic guilt and unmerited guilt as discussed previously.

It is important to recognize what degree of control you had over the event. Children obviously have no control over adult behavior. Therefore, if you are attempting to forgive childhood injuries perpetrated by an adult, the responsibility lies totally with the wrongdoer.

However, yours may be a different experience. You may have knowingly maintained an unhealthy relationship with someone whom you knew to be dangerous. You may have tolerated mistreatment when deep in your heart you knew you shouldn't. You may have avoided confrontation when confronting the person would have been appropriate. You may have enabled someone's addiction or destructive behavior by refusing to confront him or her. You may have exercised some poor judgment.

You may need to forgive yourself for exercising poor judgment. However, making a poor choice does not mean you "deserved" to be hurt. If you need to forgive yourself, do so. Review the section on forgiving yourself if you need to refresh your self-forgiveness.

Biblical Illustrations For Step Two

Step Two For Esau: Read Genesis 25:1 – 35:29

(see related questions on pages 90-91)

Esau undoubtedly wanted to blame Jacob for all his losses. How could his younger brother have pulled off such a ploy by himself? Had Rebekah, their mother, taken part in the deception? Esau may also have blamed the Lord for part of his loss. And what about his father Isaac? Wasn't he the one who sent Jacob away upon Rebekah's request, ostensibly to prevent him from marrying Hittite women? What did that mean to Esau? He had married Hittite women. Before Esau left he heard his father offer Jacob another blessing (Gen 27:46-28:5). What was that all about?

Esau may have also been confronted with the memory of his own actions. He may have recalled agreeing to sell his birthright to Jacob because he was hungry. He may have realized he *chose* to marry Hittite women (Gen 26:34-35). Was it possible that Esau's choices alienated him from both his mother and father? However, Esau probably wanted to focus the blame on Jacob. Wasn't it Jacob who had imitated him and stolen his birthright? Esau had always considered Jacob a trickster and had even nicknamed him "the grabber." Esau may have eventually concluded that Jacob was nothing more than a morally corrupt person who should be rejected, laying all the blame for his losses at Jacob's feet.

Step Two For Joseph: Read Genesis 37:1 – 50:26

Joseph may have had many people to blame for his circumstances. He may have blamed the Midianites for purchasing him and then selling him as a slave to the Egyptians. He may have harbored ill feelings towards Pharoah, Potiphar's wife, and the Cupbearer and Baker. He may have wanted to blame any and all of the people he had met, but all these others were not the ones who had betrayed him. They had not plotted against him. They had not left him for dead or sold him into slavery to strangers. These others had not abandoned him and exiled him from his home forever. No, it was his brothers, his own flesh and blood, who were responsible for his pain. Joseph must have wondered why his brothers had done this to him. Joseph may have concluded his brothers were jealous of him (Gen. 37:11).

Step Two For The Father Of The Prodigal Son: Read Luke 15:11-31

The father's struggle to identify who was responsible for his pain was different than the process for Esau or Joseph. At first glance, it may seem obvious. Who else could possibly have been responsible for his hurt other than his youngest son? But, the father may have wanted to blame others, too. The father may have wondered if an attractive young girl had lured his son away. The father may have looked at his sons' friends, or some traveler who may have whet his son's appetite for adventure by talking about far-off exotic lands. All the lad would have needed for such an adventure was money. What if the elder son had driven his younger brother away by being cruel to him? And what if, God forbid, he as the father had failed to nurture or protect the boy in the way his son needed? Why did his son do this? Why would any young man do such a thing? Did the son just want his freedom, his independence, his own life? Or, did he hate his father?

Study Guide

Step Two: Who Hurt Me And Why?

1. Read Psalm 109, and allow that Psalm to guide you in identifying those who are responsible for your hurt. Pray for clarity and discernment to identify who is responsible and what they are responsible for. This honesty will help you avoid playing the "blame game."

2. List the names of individuals who you feel hurt you. List the specific acts which you will hold him or her accountable for, and which you will eventually forgive. Be specific. Include yourself if you feel you should be on the list with a specific description of what you did and what you will eventually forgive.

Now write at the end of your list: "Although these injuries are serious, these injuries do not have to direct the rest of my life. I can choose to prevent these people and their actions from influencing any more of my life. As I forgive, I will move beyond these wounds."

Biblical Illustrations For Step Two

Step Two For Esau (Genesis 25:1-35:29)

1. What thoughts might Esau have had about his brother, mother, and father as he began to understand what happened? How might his relationships with his mother and father have changed following this event?

2. Esau might have initially concluded that Jacob stole the birthright because it was in Jacob's "grabby" nature. By doing so, Esau labels Jacob as a morally corrupt person which may alleviate some of his own responsibility. How might we label those who hurt us? What are the consequences of those labels? In labeling others, do we dehumanize them? Do we distance ourselves from responsibility?

3. Who do you think was responsible for Esau losing his blessing? Jacob? Esau? Rebekah? Issac? God? (Was it providence or divine will)?

Step Two For Joseph (Genesis 37:1-50:26)

1. Do you think that Joseph ever considered what his own contribution to his enslavement might have been? How long do you think it might have taken him to consider this?

2. Have you met people who blame everyone else for their circumstances? How do you experience these individuals? What prevents them from taking responsibility for their lives? At what point do you think Joseph began taking responsibility for his life?

Step Two For The Father Of The Prodigal Son (Luke 15:11-31)

1. If this story had literally occurred, who might the father have held accountable for his hurt? Who or what might have influenced his son's behavior? A woman? The culture? His friends? What part might the family members have played?

2. Should the father have given half his wealth to the younger son? What might have led him to do so?

3. What is your greatest hope regarding a broken relationship? What is your greatest fear?

Traveling the journey of forgiveness can challenge us to visit unfamiliar landscapes that can be uncomfortable, but it can also move us into safe and nurturing environments. In the banquet story, as the traveler opened the door and immediately smelled the aroma of food grilling, he was assured that his appetite would be satisfied. The traveler, who felt unsure and unsettled initially, felt encouragement and warmth.

Step Three: Will My
Life Ever Be The Same?

Intimate injuries can leave you feeling overwhelmed. You may feel betrayed, shocked and sometimes powerless. The world can seem out of balance. You may wonder if you will ever feel "normal" again. It is important to maintain your hope. Step Three is designed to encourage you to move beyond helplessness and to re-establish the choices you have.

Serious emotional wounds alter your life, and although this injury may feel all encompassing, it is only one small fraction of what makes you uniquely you. As you move beyond this hurt, a new sense of self will emerge. By intentionally acting to regain your emotional and spiritual footing, you will begin the process of re-establishing empowerment.

God can restore your life. But, this restoration may take time, and it will require your effort. You will need to learn to be active in the process as well as to allow God to direct your choices. God is a God of restoration. This restoration is a job for God and you to accomplish together. Naomi in the book of Ruth is a model for this restoration in the Old Testament.

Naomi

In the first chapter of the book of Ruth, we see that Naomi leaves her home place to escape famine. She starts over again in the land of Moab, only to lose her husband and her two sons to death (Ruth 1:3-18). During that ancient era, a widow with no sons or other family had no way of providing for herself. Faced with poverty, Naomi plans to return to Bethlehem, her original homeland. At Naomi's urging, her daughter-in-law Orpah leaves to return to her own family. The only constant factor in Naomi's life is Ruth, her other daughter-in-law.

So here is a woman who has lost her husband, her sons, a daughter-in-law and her home. She has no financial security and is likely expecting to live in a life of poverty. Upon returning to Bethlehem, her friends are not sure they even recognize her. Naomi's appearance has changed dramatically, likely due to all of the hardships she has endured. "Is this Naomi?" they ask when they see her (Ruth 1:19). She even claims a new name for herself: "Mara," which means "bitter" (Ruth 1:20). It appears that Naomi feels alone and abandoned by God. *I went out full but the Lord has brought me back empty.* (Ruth 1:21).

As the story unfolds, Ruth, Naomi's daughter-in-law, meets Boaz. Boaz eventually takes Ruth as his wife and in so doing redeems her and Naomi's family's inheritance. Ruth has a son, Obed, who later became the father of Jesse, who in turn became the father of David, a mighty king of Israel and ancestor to Jesus. The women around Naomi encourage her in saying *Blessed be the LORD who has not left you this day without one with the right to redeem...He shall be to you a restorer of life and a nourisher of your old age* (Ruth 4:14-15). Although Naomi's losses were devastating, she found a new home and became grandmother to a new baby boy, who is part of the Messianic line. Naomi likely continued to miss her husband and sons, but it is likely that she found new joy in her restored family. God provided Naomi with new sources of joy when she felt most destitute and abandoned. God can do the same for you.

> God provided Naomi with new sources of joy when she felt most destitute and abandoned. God can do the same for you.

How Can You Get On With Your Life? Should You Confront The Offender?

Nearly everyone who has been wounded wants to confront the person who hurt him or her. If you have fantasized about yelling and screaming at the offender, if you have imagined making him or her beg for your forgiveness, you are not alone. Many people imagine numerous ways of seeking revenge and hope for a sincere apology. Unfortunately, the apology for which they so desperately hope seldom occurs.

Confronting the offender may have a constructive purpose, although it should not be done in the spirit of revenge. The primary purpose for confronting an offender is to confront your fear of him or her. Fear and powerlessness can be paralyzing. Some individuals experience themselves one-dimensionally - as victims of the offender. For these individuals, a safe confrontation can help to form a new dimension of identity. Letting go of the role of victim and discovering one's strength can be an important step for some individuals. Beverly Flanigan refers to this process as "balancing the scales."[55]

Proving to yourself that the wrongdoer does not control your life can be important. But an actual face-to-face confrontation may not be necessary, wise or possible. There are many ways to confront your fear of the offender without a face-to-face confrontation. The person responsible may be unavailable. He or she might be aged, ill or deceased. The offender may still pose a danger to you. Confronting the offender face-to-face may not be what God is directing you to do. But you can face your fear and reassert your strength in other ways.

You may choose to stand up to the offender by writing a letter that you do not send. Writing your thoughts and feelings and reading it aloud can provide authentic empowerment. You may draw, paint or portray in some other way the process of facing up to your fear. You may have a conversation with the image of the offender.

In considering whether or not to confront the offender, we encourage you to answer the following questions:

1) How does God want me to handle this situation?

2) What exactly would I say to the offender if given the chance?

3) Do I simply want revenge?

4) Do I expect or hope for a specific response to my words? What response?

5) How would I feel if he or she did not respond in the manner I hoped? What if he or she ignored me? Denied the injury? Blamed me? Rejected me?

6) How would my relationship change with the injurer after the confrontation?

7) Are there other people who could be affected by a confrontation (children, parents, friends, loved ones)? How so?

8) What would be my ultimate purpose in confronting the injurer?

9) Are there potential consequences to a direct confrontation that I would be unwilling to live with?

10) Could I accomplish my purpose without a face-to-face confrontation?

Although there is biblical support for confronting those with whom you have grievances, we do not support the idea of confronting simply to seek revenge. In the Gospel of Matthew, Jesus speaks of *"winning your brother over,"* rather than realizing revenge. Influencing the offender's life in a positive way is another potential benefit for a face-to-face confrontation.

Jesus says, *If your brother sins against you, go and show him his fault, just between the two of you. If he listens to you, you have won your brother over. But if he will not listen, take one or two others along, so that every matter may be established by the testimony of two or three witnesses. If he refuses to listen to them, tell it to the church; and if he refuses to listen even to the church, treat him as you would a pagan or a tax collector* (Matthew 18:15-17 NIV). As you work through this process and give voice to your feelings, you will begin to feel less afraid of the offender and become reacquainted with your personal strength.

If you feel that God is guiding you to confront the offender, create a specific plan to do so with prayer and careful consideration. Talk it over with a trusted mentor, minister or counselor first. Do not act on impulse. First consider all the consequences and be prepared for any outcome. Plan when, where, and under what circumstances you will choose to confront the offender. Assure your safety and the safety of the offender. Take a firm approach but refrain from trying to intimidate or insult. Ask a safe person to be there if necessary. Allow ample time for the confrontation, but don't let it drag on indefinitely. Write out what it is you wish to say and stick to your plan. Stay calm. Above all, be clear about your intentions and be sure that God guides your actions.

As you let go of the role of victim and assert your strength, you will begin to realize God's restoration. You will discover new sources of joy.

The energy for new challenges will return and you will begin to invest yourself in new activities and relationships. You will begin to prepare to move on to the next phase on your path to forgiving the one who hurt you.

What About My Feelings Of Anger?

Abandoning your role as victim and becoming empowered will help you choose action, to move on with your life. However, you may still feel angry. You may still entertain vengeful ideas. At moments of intense anger, you may want to get even with the offender. You may want him to "pay." You may say things like, "She will pay for this. I swear she will." You may create fantasies about how to get back at him. In contrast, you may turn your anger inward and become depressed or act self destructively. You may deny or hide your anger. So what do you do with this energy - this anger?

Anger is a natural and normal reaction to being threatened or hurt. Human beings are created in the image of God with the capacity to feel anger. In many instances, anger can be right, good and appropriate, however, if anger is not expressed and dealt with appropriately, it can lead to depression, rage and violence. Furthermore, unresolved anger can cause you to relive the wound over and over in your thoughts, creating bitterness and resentment, and in turn negatively affecting your life.[56] You need to deal with your anger so you can move forward in the process of forgiveness.

Some ways to examine and communicate your feelings include studying the Bible and praying. The Bible not only gives permission to feel anger, it also offers counsel on how to express it appropriately. The Psalms are prayers of God's people and serve as a good example. They include expressions of extreme emotion, including frustration, disappointment, anger and rage. Psalm 88 is a pain-filled petition to God about the feelings of powerlessness. The psalmist cries for help while lost in the darkness. Others, including Psalm 27, 109, and 94 likewise express anger. As you read these, consider how these psalms may parallel your experience.

The psalmists and prophets are not the only biblical personalities to express anger. Remember, Jesus drives the moneychangers from the Temple and turns over tables because the "rule of God's house" has been violated (Luke 19:45-46). Jesus' anger is certainly justifiable.

God experiences anger as well. The Prophets of the Old Testament consistently portray a God who expresses wrathful anger when innocent or powerless people are oppressed or when God's will is violated or ignored. One example is from Isaiah 34:2-4,8.

The Lord is angry with all nations;
His wrath is upon all their armies.
He will totally destroy them,
He will give them over to the slaughter.
Their slain will be thrown out,
their bodies will send up a stench;
the mountains will be soaked with their blood.
All the stars of heavens will be dissolved
And the sky rolled up like a scroll;
all the starry host will fall
like withered leaves from the vine,
like shriveled figs from the fig tree.
For the Lord has a day of vengeance, a year of retribution.

The expression of anger is actually a testimony to God's care. A God who is never angry would be a God who has no compassion and empathy for those who suffer at the hands of others. Therefore, anger can very easily reveal the capacity to love.

The New Testament offers practical counsel on dealing with anger. Paul addresses the issue of anger by writing to his fellow Christians and telling them, *Be angry, but do not sin* (Ephesians 4:6). Paul continues by offering recommendations on how to deal with angry feelings, especially in relation to being lied to or deceived by someone else. First, he says, do not allow yourself to take action in destructive ways. Second, he says to deal with the anger in a timely manner. Third, he warns not to allow anger to grow into resentment, and to be reconciled with the other person if it is possible. Paul even suggests that you offer an apology for your part in the conflict, if it is appropriate. And finally, he says not to allow your anger to be turned into hostility (Ephesians 4:16-32).

In moving toward forgiveness, you must choose to deal with your anger. Give your anger to God. You can choose to sacrifice your desire to hurt or destroy others and offer those feelings to God in prayer. God can take control of them and they will no longer control you.

The Psalms and Paul's writing help you understand how to deal with anger. You are to express your anger in appropriate ways. Offer your anger to God in prayer - even if that prayer is intense shouting. Entrust your anger to God and honestly let it out. God can handle it. There are two reasons for expressing anger to God: 1) to release negative feelings in order to facilitate spiritual and emotional healing, and 2) to appeal to God's justice.

God's Justice And Divine Vengeance

The concept of vengeance comes from a number of ancient legal terms used in the Bible. Biblical vengeance is not revenge. It is not vindictiveness. It is a means for reconciling conflicts in personal relationships and the community. The prayerful cries expressed in the Psalms were cries to the Lord for redemption and restoration. And faithful people found comfort in offering their angry desires to God, and in having God announce that He would punish evil and restore His people to the fulfillment of His promises.[57]

In the New Testament, Paul offers a summary of biblical teachings on the issue of vengeance for the Christian when he declares:

> *Do not repay anyone evil for evil. Be careful to do what is right in the eyes of everybody. If it is possible, as far as it depends on you, live at peace with everyone. Do not take revenge, my friends, but leave room for God's wrath, for it is written 'Vengeance is mine,' says the Lord, 'I will repay. Therefore, if your enemy hungers, feed him, if he thirsts, give him drink for in doing so you will heap coals of fire upon his head.' Do not be overcome by evil, but overcome evil with good* (Romans 12:17-21 NIV).

It may be helpful for you to remember that God is the God of grace, but God is also the God of justice. There are two levels of accountability

99

for human injury: one is with the people involved. The other is with God. Even when you forgive someone for wounding you, that person is still accountable to God. It is that person's responsibility to make amends to God for his or her behavior. God is to be the Avenger - not you.[58]

Biblical Illustrations For Step Three

Step Three For Esau: Read Genesis 25:1-35:29
(see questions on page 103)

Esau hated Jacob and planned to kill his brother for what he had done (Gen 27:41). But Jacob was gone. There was also a growing tension between Esau and his mother. After all, she was the one who warned Jacob; *Your brother Esau is consoling himself by planning to kill you* (Gen 27:42). Esau's blood must have boiled with anger. He may have lay awake at night thinking of ways to take revenge on his brother. Esau's focus was on getting even with Jacob. He probably thought of little else; thoughts of his future were surely clouded because of his rage. And yet, Esau still continued pursuing his daily activities and comforts. He hunted and prepared stews for his family and himself. He had the love and companionship of his wives and children. Esau may have eventually come to the conclusion that he had not lost everything.

Step Three For Joseph: Read Genesis 37:1-50:26

Circumstances brought Joseph and his brothers back together (Gen 42:43-45). The brothers' mission to find food in Egypt for their desperate family members brought them face-to-face with their exiled brother.

These same circumstances afforded Joseph an opportunity for confrontation. Obviously Joseph was initially angry; but God had been good to him. He had family, wealth and power. Joseph decided to work his brothers over a little when he realized they did not recognize him (Gen 43:34). He ordered his innocent youngest brother to be brought to him and required his other brothers to make the arduous trip back to Egypt. Upon their return, he again tested them and witnessed a selflessness that had not been evident in his youth. Had Joseph's brothers changed? Had Joseph changed?

Step Three For The Father Of The Prodigal Son: Read Luke 15:11-31

The father of the wayward son was agonizing. He must have asked himself constantly "will I ever see my son again?" Everything in his life would have reminded him of the absence. The money was gone but that was incidental. The father may have lain awake at night wondering, "Where is he? Is he still alive?" Surely the father experienced raw hurt and lived with this pain hour by hour, day by day.

Summary

You have spent much energy on your journey of forgiveness. You want to be whole. You want to feel good and complete again. You now realize your anger is an acceptable part of you and that you are loved and valued by God. You also know that your anger can be turned over to God. You are ready for action.

If after reading this chapter and completing the corresponding activities in the study guide, you remain stuck in your anger, it is important to examine the origins of your feelings. Anger is understandable when you have been hurt; however, it should not be a perpetual emotion. If you find yourself stuck in your pain and anger it is possible that the current injury has fueled some feelings related to past abuse, abandonment or neglect. It may be necessary to make peace with those events before you can move on in your forgiveness.

Study Guide

Step Three - Will My Life Ever Be The Same?

1. Write a letter to the one who hurt you, expressing all your thoughts and feelings about your injury. Do not censure yourself - let it all out. **Do not send the letter.** When it is complete, read it aloud to yourself and imagine reading it to the offender. You may wish to ask a therapist, mentor or minister to listen to the letter and provide support.

2. Create a piece of art such as a drawing, painting, poem, or short story expressing your feelings and thoughts about the incident. When you work through the forgiveness process and no longer have the most intense feelings, put the work of art away.

3. Read Psalm 94 and offer it as your own prayer. Respond to these questions: What is the psalmist's complaint? What is the "sin of the wicked?" What is your complaint? How is the misuse of power or control at issue here? What part does the "lie" play?

4. Read Proverbs 20:22 NIV. *"Do not say 'I will pay you back for this wrong!' Wait for the Lord, and He will deliver you."* Pray for discernment and understanding about this proverb. Then, write a prayer that expresses your feelings about it.

5. For the next week make a daily habit of thanking God for the blessings of the day - however small these blessings seem to be at the time. Every day for one week write a brief list of at least five blessings you have received. Focus on being grateful, not on your anger or the injustices of the world.

6. Read Isaiah 34. Answer the following questions: How do you feel about these verses if you are a victim? How do you feel about these verses if you have injured someone else? Can you think of other references in scripture that help to inform the concept of "justice"?

7. Helen Bruch Pearson has written a wonderful book entitled *Do What You Have the Power to Do*. At this stage of your journey, ask yourself: "What do you have the power to do?" Can you send roses to a person who is feeling down to help their spirits? Can you donate money to the poor to assist their plight? Write in your forgiveness journal your resources, gifts, talents and abilities that you can use to focus your energy on growth instead of revenge.

Biblical Illustration For Step Three

Step Three For Esau (Genesis 25:1-35:29)

1. What feelings did Esau experience as revealed in scripture, specifically Gen 27:41?

2. How long do you think Esau's anger intruded on his life? (Remember, twenty years passed from the time of Jacob's departure until his return.) How might anger intrude on your life? What might you have to give up in order to be free of your anger? Are you confusing anger with power and control?

3. How might you need to face your fears?

Step Three For Joseph (Genesis 37:1-50:26)

1. At what point might Joseph have moved past his anger and accepted God's larger plan for his life? What needed to happen within Joseph in order for him to realize God's greater plan for him and his family?

2. What difficult experiences have you had that initially seemed meaningless, but later you came to understand them in a different light?

Step Three For The Father Of The Prodigal Son (Luke 15:11-31)

1. Imagine being the parent of a prodigal child. How might your life change following the departure of your son or daughter? At what point might your emotions shift from anger to hopefulness?

When we make a decision to accept the invitation and move toward the welcome table of forgiveness, we are motivated and challenged to see it through. We can choose to claim this sacred place as our home. It is a choice. We simply have to choose.

Step Four:
How Will I Release This Debt?

The first three steps in forgiving others are:

1. How was I hurt? How do I feel about that hurt?
2. Who is responsible for my injury? What do I feel the offender owes me?
3. Will my life ever be the same? How do I relinquish the role of victim?

When you feel you have thoroughly explored the first three steps of forgiveness, the next step includes releasing the debt. Choosing to forgive offers freedom for both you and the offender. When you forgive, you set the offender free from the debt you feel he or she owes you. This is clearly not easy to do. Human nature is first drawn to revenge. You want the offender to first suffer proportionately to your suffering, and then to restore to you what he or she took. The last thing you may want to do is set the offender free.

Releasing the offender from the debt is the act of forgiveness.

The most difficult part of the forgiveness process can be at the very beginning: to move from the desire of revenge to the desire of forgiveness. When you are ready to free yourself from the burdens of anger and resentment, you are ready to forgive. You can choose to forgive.

Consider what the offender owes you (step 2). Forgiving is letting go of the expectation that you will be repaid. Although you have every justifiable reason to continue to hold this person responsible, forgiving means setting you and this person free. Releasing the offender from the debt is the act of forgiveness.

Even if it were possible for the offender to offer full restitution, it would still be impossible for the offender to truly restore what was taken. Just as the king in Jesus' parable demonstrated, the debt you are owed cannot be repaid – but you have the power to forgive the debt. The scripture directs Christians to forgive because we are forgiven. You choose to sacrifice your desire for revenge – a part of your humanness – in order to move forward toward the freedom God provides for you through forgiveness.

The Importance Of Compassion

Through the process laid out in this book, you have worked through many emotions to arrive at this point. By reaching for and learning about forgiveness, as God in Christ has commanded, you have begun to understand yourself and others in a new way.[59] You can now honestly see things about yourself that are not perfect and still accept yourself because you know that God loves you. By acknowledging your own weakness, you become more able to accept the weakness of others. This type of understanding is compassion.

If we continually ask "What is wrong with me? What is wrong with them? Why didn't I see this coming?" we do not allow anyone to be truly human. Conversely, when we humble ourselves and accept our humanness, we can realize that at least part of our anger occurs because we are not in control, we are not omniscient (all-knowing); we are not omnipotent (all powerful). In short, we get frustrated and often hurt because we expect ourselves to be like God, when in fact, we are human with all the messiness that goes along with humanity. When we gain this insight and understanding, we are free to accept others and ourselves as finite, limited, mistake-making human beings. We then develop a greater capacity for compassion.

We are free to accept others and ourselves as finite, limited, mistake-making human beings. We then develop a greater capacity for compassion.

Scripture shows us that God is a compassionate God. Exodus 33:19 helps us understand God's choice to have compassion on humanity. God does not have to be compassionate, but God makes that *choice*.

106

And the LORD said, "I will make all my goodness pass before you, and will proclaim before you the name, the LORD, and I will be gracious to whom I will be gracious and will show mercy on whom I will show mercy."

There are many other biblical references to God's compassion, including these: *As a father has compassion for his children, so the LORD has compassion for those who fear him* (Psalm 103:13); and *But you, O Lord, are a compassionate and gracious God, slow to anger, abounding in love and faithfulness* (Psalm 86:15). [60] We are also instructed to have mercy and compassion in Zechariah: *This is what the Lord God Almighty says, "Administer true justice; show mercy and compassion to one another"* (Zechariah 7:9 NIV).

To truly love God then is to strive to be compassionate with your neighbor, even when that person hurts you, as illustrated in the Parable of the Good Samaritan (Luke 10:25-37). God in Christ illustrated compassion for you. You need also to strive to have compassion for others. You are never more like Christ than when you are compassionate to another person, especially someone who has done you harm.

Jesus teaches about compassion in Matthew 9:36, Mark 1:41, and Luke 15:20. Paul's letters continue the biblical theme of being compassionate. Colossians 3:12 says, *Therefore, as God's chosen people, holy and dearly loved, clothe yourselves with compassion, kindness, humility, meekness and patience.* Also, in Ephesians 4:32 (NIV), *Be kind and compassionate to one another, forgiving each other, just as in Christ God forgave you.*

Christ held people responsible for their actions, but his compassion was also evident. Consider the story of the woman caught in adultery in John 8:2-11. Jesus did not allow the sin committed to wipe away the hope that a sinner could repent and be forgiven. Thus, it is your challenge to identify those who have done you wrong, and see them through the hope and forgiveness that Christ offers.

These three perspectives on compassion can guide you:

- God demonstrates compassion through gracious acts toward humankind.
- We, as believers, are called to be compassionate with others.
- We, as believers, are called to be compassionate with ourselves.

No one is perfect. Everyone makes mistakes. It is part of human nature. When we as believers can honestly accept our own flaws, we can, with empathy and compassion, accept the flaws of others. Now, with empathy and compassion and in freedom you can choose to set the offender free. Then, you can be free of the painful burden of unforgiveness.

Making Your Forgiveness Concrete

Choosing to forgive is best accomplished by taking some concrete action. Marking your forgiveness in a concrete way helps you remember the moment of forgiveness. These specific actions can be thought of as forgiveness rituals or ceremonies.

Rituals help mark meaningful events in life and give order and meaning to certain events. Each person participates in an array of rituals daily. Casual rituals may include the specific way in which you get ready for your day each morning. More formal rituals include funerals and weddings.

Rituals can help give order and significance to your forgiveness. It can also help mark the moment of forgiveness in your memory. This will be important in the future should you experience fear or doubt your own forgiveness.[61] In creating a forgiveness ritual or ceremony, you are acting out your desire to release the offender from the debt he or she owes you. The offender may be part of the ritual, but does not have to be. However, if you are planning to have an intimate relationship with the wrongdoer, inviting him or her to participate in a mutual forgiveness ritual could enrich your relationship.

In this ritual, you realize the person or persons who wounded you are to blame, but you declare that you no longer expect any repayment from the offender. You also declare before God that you forgive the one who hurt you, just as God forgives you through Jesus' sacrifice. In forgiving, you relinquish your preoccupation with the injury and the one who caused it and deliberately focus on your future. You free yourself from the weight of resentment and move on with hope. It may sound simple, but it is a crucial step in freeing yourself from unforgiveness.

When you forgive the offender, you no longer expect anything from him. You do not desire money, or time, or even an explanation. You are aware of the biblical mandate to forgive as you recognize that forgiveness is in your own best interest. You choose to forgive. With this decision, the ultimate scales of justice swing in your favor. As you choose to release bad feelings and bad memories, you realize that the greatest blessing of forgiveness goes to the one who forgives.

As mentioned earlier, it is important to determine a concrete way to accomplish these critical tasks of forgiveness. You may begin in prayer by writing a letter to God and asking for help in accomplishing these tasks. Ask God for specific help in forgiving.

When you have asked for help from God and are ready to forgive, it is time to write a letter to the offender. This letter is not to be sent, but will allow you an opportunity to express your forgiveness honestly without any need to censure yourself.

In your letter, tell the offender in your own words that you release him or her from the debt caused by the injury. Let him know you no longer expect any restitution. Tell the offender that you are forgiving, just as you have been forgiven. Let him know that you will no longer think of yourself in terms of victim, but rather as a strong survivor with more abilities now than in the past. Write that you will no longer define yourself in terms of the event, but instead define yourself in terms of your "God-Worth". Describe how you are moving on with your life. Define the boundaries of any future relationship you will have with this person (which may include much or little distance). Write the words "Just as I have been forgiven, I forgive you and I release you from the debt you owe me." Add anything else to the letter that you feel is necessary.

After you have written the letter and feel it is complete, read it aloud at least three times. Now spend some time with God in prayer. Offer your forgiveness to God as a way of deepening your commitment to God. Tell God of your choice and thank God for the forgiveness that you have received. Tell God that you no longer choose to define yourself in terms of this event, but rather will now think of yourself in terms of your relationship with God. You may choose to offer this prayer as part of a religious ceremony such as Holy Communion, or may pray it in solitude with God. Note your forgiveness in your journal, to be referred to as many times as needed. Keep the letter as a reminder of your choice to forgive and be free.

Biblical Illustrations For Step Four

Step Four For Esau: Read Genesis 25:1-35:29

(See related questions on pages 113-114)

Esau may have forgiven Jacob long before the younger brother made his way back over the River Jabbok. He may have through time, introspection and prayer made peace with the debt that Jacob owed him. But when Esau received Jacob's messengers (32:1-7) and gifts (32:19-20), he must have interpreted this as Jacobs's confession and repentance. Esau went to meet his brother with 400 men and Jacob was terrified. Jacob prayed to God to be delivered from Esau (32:11).

Jacob was preparing for the confrontation of his life. He knew Esau swore to kill him, and he knew he deserved Esau's wrath (32:9-11). But, Esau approached Jacob with a different agenda. Esau had apparently made peace with Jacob's deception and debt. Why and how? Had Esau gained knowledge and understanding and processed his own feelings? Had Rebekah shared with her eldest son that God had announced to her before his birth the destiny of her two sons? Was Esau happy and content with his Hittite wives and wealth and daily hunting trips? Was Esau even concerned about things like "chosen-ness" or "blessings" or "birthrights"? It appears that Esau had matured, grown and forgiven.

The biblical narrative tells us that Esau had everything he ever wanted or needed and more. So, in Esau's view, he had recovered from the loss of his birthright and moved beyond the hurt. The stolen blessing that he thought was critically important had not robbed him of anything he wanted or valued. The entire event had cost him very little - except the presence of his twin brother. And Esau probably reflected and realized, as he roamed the hillsides hunting for game, that his brother was not perfect - and neither was he.

Step Four For Joseph: Read Genesis 37:1-50:26

Joseph's present life is wonderful. His future is unbelievably bright. But here comes the past. Although the reunion with his family is wonderful to Joseph, the hurt from the past returns to him. Joseph has had time to reflect on his entire life. He has gained an awareness and insight into his own behavior. Perhaps he could have related to his brothers differently when he was young. Perhaps his arrogance, intelligence, and his dreams had annoyed them. Perhaps his years as a slave and prisoner had taught him some humility. He learned about fear as a youngster. Now, he has taught his family about that emotion. His family is afraid: afraid of starvation and afraid of him. He confronts his brothers by revealing himself to them. And then he reinterprets the entire event that happened so many years ago. He shares with them his understanding of the blessings and good that God has made out of what was once a tragedy (45:5).

Step Four For The Father Of The Prodigal Son: Read Luke 15:11-31

The father waits. He longs for his sons return. He waits patiently. He spends his time preparing for the meeting with his son, premeditating every word he will say and every movement he will make. He might imagine the moment that his son will crest the hill. If he is ever blessed enough to see his younger son come down the road that leads to his home he will be prepared. Patiently and painfully, the father waits.

Study Guide

Step Four – How Will I Release This Hurt?

1. Your choice to forgive needs to be accompanied by a specific act of forgiveness. In addition to the letter you may write, you may choose to demonstrate your forgiveness in other ways. Consider the acts of forgiveness listed below:

> a. Write a short description of the debt you are forgiving and tie it to a helium balloon. As the balloon floats away, allow your unforgiveness to float away.

> b. Participate in a service of The Lord's Supper or Holy Communion. As you take part in the banquet meal, go to the altar and leave a symbol of the debt at the cross of Christ.

> c. Place a description of the debt in a small box and bury it, allowing it to symbolize the death of the debt and your forgiveness. (This may be particularly helpful if you are forgiving someone who has died.)

2. Study Proverbs 20:22 (NIV): *Do not say, "I'll pay you back for this wrong." Wait for the Lord, and he will deliver you.* Consider how this statement captures your feelings of anger and attempts to be compassionate. Write a prayer that expresses your feelings about this proverb.

3. Read the scriptures below and consider the following questions: What does the scripture say about God's compassion? What does the scripture say about the biblical expectation of human compassion? What does the scripture say about the relationship between God's compassion and our compassion?

> a. Isaiah 49:15 (NIV) – *Can a mother forget the baby at her breast and have no compassion on the child she has borne? Though she may forget, I will not forget you.*

b. Psalm 103:13 – *As a father has compassion for his children, so the Lord has compassion for those who fear him.*

c. Ephesians 4:32 (NIV) – *Be kind and compassionate to one another, forgiving each other, just as in Christ God forgave you.*

4. Reverend Dr. John Patton says, "Human forgiveness is impossible." How do you interpret this statement based on your experience and understanding of forgiveness?

Biblical Illustrations For Step Four

Step Four For Esau (Genesis 25:1-35:29)

1. What might have been Esau's thoughts when he first encountered Jacob's messengers? What might have been his motivation to take 400 men with him to meet Jacob?

2. In what ways might Esau have matured in the years since Jacob's flight? Might Esau put less stock in the concept of "chosen-ness"? How might such issues be reflected in our culture today?

3. Do you think forgiveness becomes easier as Christians mature in their faith? How so?

Step Four For Joseph (Genesis 37:1-50:26)

1. What insights might Joseph have developed during the decades of separation from his family? How might experiences have afforded Joseph a new perspective? What experiences have you had that have helped you gain new perspectives about difficult situations?

2. How does Joseph reinterpret what were once tragic life-changing events (Gen. 45:5)? What might believers glean from Joseph's insight?

Step Four For The Father Of The Prodigal Son (Luke 15:11-31)

1. What was the father's immediate reaction to the sight of his starving son traveling toward home?

2. What might have been the son's attitude and posture at seeing his father for the first time? Do you believe the son's repentance was genuine? What experiences did the son have which helped him "come to his senses"? How difficult might it have been for the son to seek forgiveness?

3. If the son had not been repentant, do you think the father would have been so overjoyed to see him?

It takes courage to come this far in the journey of forgiveness. It takes courage to leave the familiar and venture into new places emotionally and spiritually. How has this journey changed us? How do we look now that we are wearing the mantle of courageous adventurers? What will we do now?

Step Five:
Who Will I Now Become?

As you leave behind the role of victim, you will begin to glimpse your restored self. You will experience a renewed interest in outside activities and have more energy to pursue those interests. This is a time to assess who you will become and make some intentional choices about where your life will go from here. In becoming a new creature, you have three tasks before you:

1. Affirm that you are God's treasure
2. Create intentional and concrete plans
3. Follow through with those plans

Affirm That You Are God's Treasure

Being wounded can cause you to question your value, especially if that wound involves rejection. When you are rejected, your self-confidence can erode. After an injury, self-blame and shame can eat away at self-worth. Therefore, following an injury, it is important to acknowledge your value as a child of God. You are inherently valuable. You are a treasure in God's eyes. It makes no difference how people treat you or what others think of you. But even the most precious treasure can be damaged and be in need of refinement. And when a valued treasure is refined, regardless if it is an antique solid mahogany table, or a gold bracelet, or you, it becomes like new again. Now is the time to reflect on how much God treasures you.

More than one hundred verses in the Bible refer to God's delight in his people (see Zephaniah 3:17 as an example). Allow yourself to be thankful in God's delight. Thank God for delighting in all creation, including you, and recommit to viewing yourself through the forgiving lens of Jesus' sacrifice.

Create Intentional And Concrete Plans

As you heal from your wounds, you will most likely spend less and less of your energy coping with the past and begin focusing more energy on the present and future. You will discover more energy for interests and activities in your life. This is the time to take stock of what is important to you and examine the direction you would like your life to go from this point forward.

Ask yourself the following questions:

- What do I need to do to demonstrate to myself that I am moving beyond the injury?
- What is most important to me in my life? What do I value most?
- Does my life reflect what is most important to me? Do I need to arrange my life such that I focus on what is most important?
- What specific plans do I want to make for my future that will reflect my values and my restored self?

For example, if you place a high value on developing and building your faith, you may choose to renew your commitment to a church, join a Bible study or find a regular prayer partner. If your family and loved ones are central in your life, you may need to spend more time with those you love. If community involvement is one of your core values, you may commit to volunteer within your community.

It is now important to make intentional choices about your future. Seek God's guidance for what your plans should be. Ask God to guide your choices in demonstrating your new stronger forgiving and forgiven self. Seek God's blessing.

Many individuals mistakenly think that forgiveness simply puts things back the way they were before the injury occurred. Rather, reconciliation is a restoration of harmony in your life

Reconciliation that comes with true forgiveness always brings change.

and with those around you. Reconciliation is not a return to the way things were. The reconciliation that comes with true forgiveness always brings change. The change will include new and different perspectives, relationships and understandings.

There will be changes in some relationships, particularly if you have

117

a relationship with the offender. This change may involve establishing a new closeness along with new boundaries or rules. Changes may include distancing from old ways and former relationships, and guarding your well-being through healthy patterns and strong boundaries. And the change will need to include a more intimate relationship with God.

Following Through With Plans

Lay out a blueprint for your future that demonstrates your forgiveness and readiness to proceed with your restored life. After you have assessed your new values and drafted your plan, get out a calendar and set a date to act on your plan. Ask someone in your life to serve as your accountability partner with whom you will report your progress. This may be a friend, mentor, therapist or minister; but tell someone of your intentions. Also, make your plans part of your prayer life. Tell God of your plans and ask for direction.

As your plans unfold, you will move beyond the injury and toward becoming a new creature. You will be stronger because you have allowed God to use the injury to strengthen your faith and your ability to cope with trials.

As a new creation blessed by God's grace, consider identifying with a magnanimous king who forgave a "wicked servant" an impossible debt. You have now fulfilled the challenge that Christ posed to Peter and the disciples, to be like the king in the parable (Matthew 18:20-35), and to *forgive your brother or sister from your heart.*

Therefore, as you commit (and recommit when necessary) to forgiving and offer your hurts and anger as a sacrifice to God, you become refined, a new being, better able to serve God. Your relationships are different, with new and more informed perspectives, and new and safer boundaries. You are a new creation! Rejoice and be glad in it!

Biblical Illustrations For Step Five

Step Five For Esau: Read Genesis 25:1-35:29

(See related questions on pages 122-123)

Scripture tells us that Jacob became a new person on his journey to reconcile with Esau. *You shall no longer be called Jacob, but Israel for you*

118

have striven with God and with humans and have prevailed (Gen. 32:28). But Jacob is also blessed with new beginnings when he encounters Esau. Jacob is terrified as he approaches his older brother. *But, Esau ran to meet him, and embraced him, and fell on his neck and kissed him, and they wept* (Gen. 33:4). Jacob tries to pay for his past sins, but Esau says, *I have enough* (Gen. 33:10). Jacob's response, *No please, if I find favor with you, then accept my present from my hand, for truly to see your face is like seeing the face of God – since you have received me with such favor.*

Esau is a new person, too. Jacob, while maybe not consciously aware of it, feels blessed and Esau has embraced his past misfortune in the same way he now embraces his younger brother. The two estranged brothers are reunited. But this forgiveness will not include a reconciliation that means the two brothers will live together happily ever after.

Their reconciliation will mean they will be emotionally reunited, and not focus on the events of the past, but they will go their separate ways, living a safe distance from each other. Love and peace between the brothers has been restored (Genesis 33:15-17).

Step Five For Joseph: Read Genesis 37:1-50:26

Joseph and his family are reunited. Their relationships are restored. Joseph took care of his father and brothers and their families. He has blessed them even as he has been blessed. Everything seems fine until their father Jacob's death.

In the closing scene of the story, the repentant brothers approach Joseph with a little manipulated appeal of their own. When Jacob dies, Josephs' brothers become fearful that he will now take revenge on them. They tell Joseph that Jacob's dying desire was for him to take care of them. Joseph's response is one of grace and absolution: *Do not be afraid. Am I in the place of God? Even though you intended harm to me, God intended it for good, in order to preserve a numerous people* (Gen. 50:19-20). Joseph's forgiveness is clear. He is reconciled to his brothers and he assures them of his forgiveness.

Interestingly, Joseph's forgiveness does not automatically give his brothers the experience of being forgiven. They have not been able to receive his forgiveness at this point. They may not have forgiven themselves for selling Joseph into slavery. They do not trust Joseph because they may be dealing with guilt and shame themselves. As the biblical account closes, we can only assume that the brothers have more work to do regarding forgiveness.

Step Five For The Father Of The Prodigal Son: Read Luke 15:11-31

The father has been waiting with hope beyond hope. Then he sees his son coming down the road. The father runs and embraces his son before the son even has time to deliver his remorseful lines, *Father, I have sinned against heaven and against you. I am no longer worthy to be called your son; make me like one of your hired men* (Luke 15:21 NIV). The father is filled with compassion. He throws his arms around his son and kisses him (Luke 15:20b). The father quickly offers directives that he has been planning for just such an occasion. He tells the servants, *Quickly! Bring out a robe – the best one – and put it on him; put a ring on his finger and sandals on his feet. And get the fatted calf and kill it, and let us eat and celebrate; for this son of mine was dead and is alive again; he was lost and is found. So they began to celebrate* (Luke 15:22-24).

The younger son has returned. His words and presence are a confession and a true repentance. The father's embrace and call for celebration are a dramatic portrayal of reconciliation. Their relationship is restored. We do not know how things will be different with the father and the younger son, but they are together again.

Someone else in the family is not ready to forgive the wayward son. The elder son is angry (Luke 15:28) and filled with resentment. Even the father's explanations and pleas for him to accept his younger brother do not move the older son (Luke 15:31-32).

Reconciliation between the father and the younger son does not mean forgiveness and reconciliation for the older brother. He resents his younger brother. He is concerned about issues of fairness and justice. As the parable closes, the impression is left that forgiveness remains an issue for the older brother.

Study Guide

Step Five: Who Will I Now Become?

1. Read silently Psalm 96. Re-read it out loud. Then offer it as a personal prayer. Now, rewrite the Psalm in your own words, putting each phrase in your own words. Can you "sing to the Lord a new song?"

2. Read the paraphrase below of Psalm 91 from *Psalms Now!* by Lezslie F. Brandt. Does this Psalm help you reflect on your journey of forgiveness? If so, what thoughts do you have about this Psalm, and how does it speak to you?

> *The one whose faith is focused on God,*
> *Who finds security in Him, does not have to live in fear.*
> *He is not left untouched by the tempests of this life,*
> *And he may be wounded by the onslaughts of evil,*
> *But his great God does not leave him to suffer these things alone.*
> *The Lord cares for his own and delivers him even in the midst of*
> *the conflicts that plague him.*
>
> *If God is truly your God, you do not have to be afraid of the*
> *enemy that threatens the affliction that lays you low.*
> *Men all about you may fall, never to rise again,*
> *but the Lord is by your side to raise you to your feet and to lead*
> *you to ultimate victory.*
>
> *Even the ministering spirits of His invisible world are watching*
> *over you.*
> *They will not allow anything to hurt you except by God's loving*
> *permission and through His eternal concern.*

Our loving God has promised it:
Because my child loves Me, I will never let him go.
I shall feel the pain of his wounds and bear his hurt
and shall transform that which is ugly into that which enriches
and blesses.
And when he cries out in agony, I shall hear and answer him.
I will be close to him and will deliver him, and I will grant
him eternal life.

3. Romans 12:2 reads: *Do not be conformed to this world, but be transformed by the renewing of your minds, so that you may discern what is the will of God – what is good and acceptable and perfect.* List some of the gifts you realize you now possess as a result of your journey to forgiveness. In what ways have you been transformed? In what ways have you been restored?

Biblical Illustrations For Step Five

Step Five For Esau (Genesis 25:1-35:29)

1. How did Esau change? How did he demonstrate that change? Read Genesis 33.

2. How did Jacob change? How did he demonstrate that change? When Esau welcomed Jacob home, how might that have cemented these changes for Jacob? Read Genesis 33.

3. How did the brothers demonstrate and negotiate their reconciliation?

Step Five For Joseph (Genesis 37:1-50:26)

1. Read Genesis 50:15-20. What does this scripture illustrate about Joseph's forgiveness and maturity in God?

2. Why do you think Joseph's brothers were afraid, even after he had assured them of his forgiveness?

3. Do you think someone you forgive may not genuinely receive your forgiveness? Why? Could you say or do anything to convince them of your forgiveness? What?

Step Five For The Father Of The Prodigal Son (Luke 15:11-31)

1. Read Luke 15:22-24. How might the father's reaction have helped to solidify the prodigal's remorse? How might the father's reaction have been a catalyst for the son to change?

2. Read Luke 15:28. What was the older son's reaction to the forgiveness freely offered to the younger son? Why was he so offended? How might Christians' behavior often reflect that of the older son? Why do you think this is so?

Final Thoughts On Forgiving Others

So, how do you know that you have forgiven someone? There is a simple test: If you genuinely and sincerely pray for blessings for the offender, you have forgiven him or her.

Your experience of becoming a new person may not be quite as dramatic as that of Naomi, or Joseph, or the Prodigal Son. But you are a new creation. And just as Jacob became Israel in his journey, so you also are a new creation, because you, too, have *wrestled with God and with man and have prevailed* (Genesis 32:24).

And so the ledger on the economy of forgiveness is closed. As Paul says in Romans 13:8, *Owe no one anything, except to love one another; for the one who loves another has fulfilled the law.*

We now invite you to join the mission of delivering the message of God's grace and love and forgiveness to all those who have not heard it. It is the same mission that Paul wrote to the Corinthians, *[We are called to] spread the fragrance of the knowledge of Jesus everywhere* (II Cor. 2:14-16).

At times along the journey of forgiveness, we may wonder, "Why did God create all these dark places and harsh landscapes?" "Why are there dangerous places and devastating experiences ready to cause us harm?" "Why do trusted loved ones hurt us?" Just as the traveler in the story realized, Christ sits at the same table we do. Christ also experienced devastation, loneliness, betrayal, and finally murder. Although we usually don't fully realize it at the beginning of our journey, we have a God that loves us enough to go through these dark places with us.

Circle Four:
Dealing with Issues with
God Following a Loss

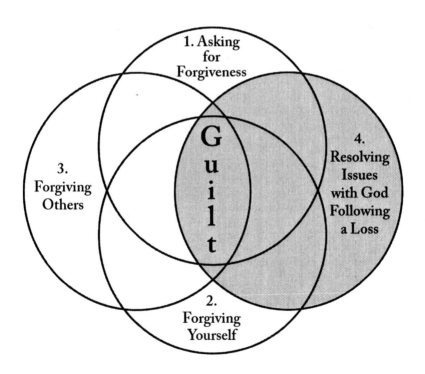

What If I Am Angry With God?

A serious injury can cause you to question everything in your life. A serious injury can make you angry with God. You may have prayed that God would prevent or heal your injury and feel your prayers went unanswered. You may feel guilty and think there is some reason God is punishing you. You may feel abandoned by God and cry out, "Where are you, God?" You may blame God because God did not prevent the injury.

You search for some reasonable explanation for your injury. You try to make the incident make sense. When there is no reasonable explanation, it can be easy to blame God. After all, God set the universe in motion. God created people. Your anger with God is understandable.

First, realize that you are not the first person to cry out "why?" or to express anger at God. The psalmist cried out. Job cried out. Even Jesus cried out from the cross, *My God, my God, why have you forsaken me?* (Mark 15:34). Abraham, Moses, Samuel, David, Elijah, Jeremiah, Peter and Paul all expressed anger, frustration, disagreement or disappointment at various times in their relationship with God.

Second, know that God is bigger than all of your anger. Your anger will not harm God.

Third, You are angry with God, so tell God. Express your anger in your prayers. Put your feelings into words. This may lead to a closer relationship with God. However, it is important to examine closely what is behind your feelings of abandonment or anger. When you were injured, your world turned upside down. Your trust was betrayed. What you presumed to be true and just and fair about the world collapsed. And perhaps God failed to meet your expectations. Being aware of this will lead you to a healthier and more mature spiritual perspective. Your anger at God can provide an opportunity for you to grow in your understanding of yourself and in your relationship with God.

Individual expectations can cause you trouble in human relationships as well as in your relationship with God. Expectations are formed from our early experiences. For example, images of a benign, gift-giving, grandfatherly man may have been one of your earliest images of God. If you do not spiritually mature beyond that image, then God will disappoint you when you ask for something and don't get it. Many other images that we develop are reflections of human characteristics or traits of people we know and experience.[62] We are tempted, however innocently and unaware, to fashion God into our own images and likenesses.[63]

If you are angry and frustrated at God because God has not met an expectation and has disappointed you, then allow this event to help you understand God in a new way. As you do so, you will be better equipped to deal with your anger. Your faith will grow as you reflect on these old images of God and explore new ones.

Hold on to your faith. God is with you in these feelings and expressions of anger. They are actually expressions of faith that will help you grow spiritually. This process can help you relinquish false or immature images of faith and move into a more mature understanding of God.

How Do You Explore Your Image Of God?

Your initial exploration should include the scriptures. The Bible portrays God in vastly different images that challenge childhood understanding: the strangers who visit Abraham and Sarah with an unexpected birth announcement (Gen. 18:1-15); an unnamed man who wrestles all night with Jacob (Gen. 32:22-31); the fourth man in the furnace with Daniel's friends (Dan. 3:1-30). You might consider what it means for the Bible to describe God as a devouring lion (Hosea 13:6-9); a shade tree and fruitful tree (Hosea 14:4-7); the *Word* (John 1:1), or even like maggots and infection in an open sore (Hosea 5:12). And in John 4:24, Jesus declares, *"God is Spirit."*

God's most faithful servants were challenged by how they experienced God. As Elijah hid in a cave in fear, he expected God to show up with great force: as a brilliant fire, as an earthquake, or as a whirlwind. But a "still small voice" revealed the warmth and intimacy of the presence of God (I Kings 19:9-18). Elijah had to release his expectations and change his mind about God. And Mary, weeping alone in the Garden after having found no body in the tomb had lost all hope. When she heard her name called by someone standing behind her in the garden, she assumed it was the gardener. But it was the resurrected Jesus, revealing himself to her and transforming her into a joy-filled messenger of hope for the world (John 20:10-18).

127

Mary's perspective was so dramatically altered she gained an entirely new vision of reality. Like Elijah and Mary, adopting different perspectives is never easy, but it's an important step in growing through your anger with God. Evaluate your notions of who you expect God to be and compare them to the true nature of God.

For the Christian there is no greater revelation of God than the person of Jesus Christ. Although God may not suspend the laws of nature to spare you from harm, God does not intentionally harm you. Instead, God empathizes with your suffering through the person of Christ. God, in Christ, experienced the essence of your vulnerability through His earthly experiences. Friends disappointed Jesus (see Matthew 26:17-35); he lost people for whom he cared (Jesus' friend Lazarus dies, John 11); he was maligned and tortured (Mark 15:15-20); and finally he was murdered as a criminal. Even at the moment of his death, his words reveal his momentary powerlessness (Mark 22:34). Christ was not spared from pain; nor are you. God never promised you would escape from pain. Instead, God through Christ suffers along with all humanity. The God of the Bible is not the enemy of hurting people, but their hope.

The realizations gained from scripture about God can be humbling. As you gain an insight about who God is, you gain understanding from the Scripture:

> *"For my thoughts are not your thoughts, neither are your ways my ways," declares the LORD. "As the heavens are higher than the earth, so are my ways higher than your ways and my thoughts than your thoughts"* (Isaiah 55:8).

When you realize that the Living God is not neatly contained in any humanly conceived box (or tomb), you are better prepared to gain a response to your unanswered "why" question. Like Job, you can come to realize that your cry to God is answered, not by a verbal response, but by experiencing God's presence through Jesus and the Holy Spirit.

The most concrete way for you to experience and commune with God is in prayer. But, you may not know how to pray: you may feel too angry to pray. If you feel like you don't want to pray, talk with a minister, a Christian spiritual director, or...just pray! Sometimes you may think God does not hear you. As with any relationship you will gain understanding as you get to know God better. You will get to know God better through Bible study, prayer, meditation and the presence of the Holy Spirit in fellowship and in worship with other Christians. The Psalmist prayed, *"Show me your ways, O LORD, teach me your paths"* (Psalm 25:4). May that be your prayer as well.

Allow the Holy Spirit to challenge the way you think about things, broadening or deepening your perspective. Grow in your understanding. You will come to know God in moments of pain and suffering. You will come to know God as the one who heals and consoles, refreshes and sustains. As you grow you can declare with Paul:

> *Where there is knowledge, it will pass away.*
>
> *For we know in part and we prophesy in part,*
>
> *but when perfection comes the imperfect disappears.*
>
> *When I was a child, I talked like a child, I thought like a child,*
>
> *I reasoned like a child.*
>
> *When I became an adult, I put childish ways behind me.*
>
> *Now we see but a poor reflection as in a mirror;*
>
> *then we shall see face to face.*
>
> *Now I know in part; then I shall know fully;*
>
> *even as I am fully known* (I Cor. 13:8-12 NIV).

Study Guide

What If I Am Angry With God Following A Loss?

1. Make a list of your images of God. What images come to mind? Try to identify where those images came from. Who do you think of when you think of God?

Make a list of the characteristics you attribute to God. How many are from the Bible? How many are from other sources? How might these images form your beliefs and expectations of how God should act?

William and Christi Gaultiere, in their book *Mistaken Identity,* offer several images of God that borrow from biblical sources that are usually taken out of context. Some of the images are Elitist Aristocrat, Magic Genie, Demanding Drill Sergeant, Dictator, Party Pooper, and Critical Scrooge. Have you ever thought of God in these terms?

2. Do you tend to blame God for events in your life? Do you tend to think that other events or forces are responsible? Some people believe that God tests or punishes us. Others believe that all misfortune is due to Adam and Eve. Others believe that the devil is the author of all tragedy. How have you come to understand the source of sadness in your life?

3. Offer honest prayers to God regarding your pain. Simply tell God that you do not understand and that you are frustrated. If you are angry or sad, tell God what you are feeling. If you have a sense of loss, express that to God. Share your tears and sadness with God. (As one author put it, "God gave us tears to wash away pain and to cleanse our memories.")

Offer this prayer, or one similar to it:

Dear Lord, I do not think I have it in me to forgive what has been done to me. You know my pain. You know the hurt that is in my heart. But I am also burdened by the words of Your Son. He has told me to forgive the very person who has hurt me so deeply.

I feel the desire for revenge, but I wish to choose His way. Make me, a vulnerable human being, a vessel for Your love and understanding. Heal me as Your forgiveness passes through me to others. I praise You and thank You, merciful Lord. Amen

Endnotes

1   Patton, J. *Is Human Forgiveness Possible?* 158

2   Matthew 28:20b, John 15:4-14, John 14:15-21.

3   To learn more about specific examples of these sacrifices study chapter four of the Book of Leviticus.

4   *Webster's New World Compact School and Office Dictionary*, 1989, 27

5   Matt. 18:23-25.

6   Erikson, E. *Childhood and Society*, 247.

7   Schneider, *Shame, Exposure and Privacy*, 20.

8   Patton, J. *Is Human Forgiveness Possible?*, 43.

9   Kaufman, G. *Shame: The Power of Caring*, 85-101.

10 Patton, J. *Forgiveness in Pastoral Care and Counseling*, In M. McCullough, et. al., *Forgiveness: Theory, Research, and Practice.* 286.

11 Patton, J. *Is Human Forgiveness Possible*, 54-59.

12 Buber, M. *Good and Evil* "Psalms 12", 7.

13 Smalley, G. & Trent, J., *The Blessing*, 125

14 Brueggemann, W., *Genesis: Interpretation Bible Commentary*, 49

15 Armstrong, K., *In the Beginning*, 30

16 Patton, J, *Is Human Forgiveness Possible?* 65-116.

17 See Genesis 37:3, 23, 32; II Corinthians 5:4.

18 Smedes, L., *Shame and Grace.* 83.

19 Smedes, L., *Shame and Grace*, 80.

20 Smedes, L., *Shame and Grace*, 126.

21 See Genesis 1:10, 12, 18, 21

22 See Exodus 33:18-20; Psalms 17:7-8; 145:8-14.

23 The word translated as humility is a profound biblical image. Taken from the word "hummus," it means earthy, lowly, real.

24   The *Lex Taliones* is the biblical implementation of an ancient code of retaliation based on a guilty party receiving the same injury that they visited upon an innocent party. Biblical examples can be found in Deuteronomy 19:21 "Show no pity: life for life, eye for eye, tooth for tooth, hand for hand, foot for foot," Exodus 21:24 "eye for eye, tooth for tooth, hand for hand, foot for foot,," Levi 24:20 "fracture for fracture, eye for eye, tooth for tooth; the injury inflicted is the injury to be suffered," and Matt 5:38 (NRSV) "You have heard that it was said, 'An eye for an eye and a tooth for a tooth.'"

25   Levites were the descendents of Levi, the son of Jacob, commissioned by God through Moses to oversee the religious/political activities of the tribes of Israel.

26   Yancy, P., *What's so Amazing About Grace?*, 137-138.

27   Telushkin, Rabbi Joseph, *Jewish Literacy*, 541-542. Jewish believers observe this practice of confession annually during the Holy Days of Rosh ha-Shana. During these days, the Jewish believer is encouraged to confess her wrong doings to those whom she has harmed and seek forgiveness. The Holy Days conclude with the Jewish High Holy Day of Atonement. The Day of Atonement is designed for Jewish believers to spend some time in public and private prayer seeking reconciliation with God. This Jewish tradition emphasizes the importance of confession and restoration among the community as well as with God.

28   Flanigan, B., *Forgiving Yourself,* 125.

29   The biblical concept of "contrition" holds that a Christian genuinely has sorrow in her heart, detests the act that she committed, and is resolved to sin no more. This spirit is required, in Christian tradition, before confession is made. Then there is a strong desire to "make things right" with the person you have injured. You are motivated to make reparation, as far as is humanly possible, for the wrong you have done. Without this mindset, confession means nothing. This is true in our relationship with God, with others, and with ourself.

30   Other biblical references related to confession can be found in Leviticus 5:5, Mark 1:4-5, and James 5:16.

31   Jesus said, "So when you are offering your gift at the altar, if you remember that your brother or sister has something against you, leave your gift there before the altar and go; first be reconciled to your brother or sister, and then come and offer your gift. Come to terms quickly with your accuser while you are on the way to court with him, or your accuser may hand you over to the judge, and the judge to the guard, and you will be thrown into prison. Truly I tell you, you will never get out until you have paid the last penny" (Matt 5:23-26).

32   Dunham, M., *Workbook on Spiritual Disciplines*, 68

33   We are using the principle of *confession* to include both confessing and/or admission – admitting our wrongs to someone we have wounded. To distinguish between them, we will identify confession as coming from an accused conscience; admission is what happens after one gets caught.

34   Madnes, C., *Love, Sex and Violence*, 53

35   Winmill Brown, W., Ed., *The Martyred Christian: 160 Readings from Dietrich Bonhoeffer*, 64.

36   Other Biblical references to repentance can be found in Ezekiel 14:6, Mark 1:4, and Acts 2:38.

37   For more on identifying personal limitation or flaws see *Forgiving Yourself* by Beverly Flanigan.

38   Remember how the people of Nineveh in the Book of Jonah (3:5-9) humbled themselves and repented in prayer and fasting when confronted with their sins, and God dealt graciously with them.

39   Read II Corinthians 5:19-20 and Romans 5:10 for more perspective on reconciliation.

40   Note: If we are honest with ourselves, many can probably identify closely with the older brother, who obviously resented his Father's reaction to the younger brother's return. Many scholars believe the original intent of this parable was to teach the Jewish community about God's grace – they too were to identify with the older brother.

41   For other scripture references regarding God's compassion read II Kings 13:23 and Psalm 145:9.

42 Madanes, C., *Love, Sex and Violence*, 54.

43 Flanigan, B., *Forgiving Yourself*, 59.

44 For more information about self –forgiveness, see *Forgiving Yourself* by Beverly Flanigan.

45 Smedes, L., *Forgive and Forget*, 99.

46 A clergy person may be able to help you identify appropriate expressions of penance as work to forgive yourself and accept God's forgiveness of you. The Christian tradition has many formalized and informal rituals to make such expression.

47 United Methodist Book of Worship, "Service of Word and Table I, Confession and Pardon," (Nashville, Tennessee: The United Methodist Publishing House, 1992) 35.

48 Merrill, N. C., *Meditations and Mandalas: Simple Songs for the Spiritual Life*, 76.

49 Tennen, H. & Affleck, G., *Blaming Others for Threatening Events*. Psychology Bulletin, 209-232.

50 Enright, R. 2001. *Forgiveness is a Choice; A Step-By-Step Process for Resolving Anger and Restoring Hope*, 53-54.

51 McCraty,R., Atkinson, M., Tiller, W., Rein, G., & Watkins, A., *The Effects of Emotions on Short Term Power Spectrum Analysis on Heart Rate Variability*, 1089-1093.

52 Coyle, C.T. & Enright, R.D., 1042-1046. Freedmon , S.R. & Enright, R.D., 983-992.

53 Flanigan, B. *Forgiving the Unforgivable*, 31. Flanigan's list of "unforgivable" acts include: abuse (both physical and mental); abandonment; infidelity; loss of money, job or reputation; loss of health or life; and loss of freedom.

54 Smedes, L., *Forgive and Forget*, 44.

55 Flanigan, B., *Forgiving the Unforgivable*, 124.

56 Enright, R. (2001). *Forgiveness is a Choice: A Step-by-Step Process for Resolving Anger and Restoring Hope*, 53-54.

57 There are many references in Scripture to illustrate this point. For example, Psalm 58 is a faithful petition to God to carry out vengeance against evil leaders. Also see, Deuteronomy 32:32-46; Isaiah 34:8; 47:3; 63:3-8; Ezekiel 25:17; Luke 21:22; II Thessalonians 1:8.

58 In a sense, revenge is *irreverent*. When we strike back at someone who injured us we are saying, 'I know vengeance is yours God, but I just didn't think you'd punish him enough. You may be a little soft on him."

59 When we acknowledge the limits of others we can empathize with them. Empathy has been found to be a necessary component of forgiveness. Scholars have found empathy to be consistently present in people who can forgive. For more read McCullough, M.E., Worthington, E.L, & Rachal, K.C. "Interpersonal Forgiving in Close Relationships." *Journal of Personality and Social Psychology*, Vol. 73, 1997, 321-336.

60 Other scripture references about God's compassion include: Deut 13:17; 2 Kings 13:23; Psalm 145:9; Psalm 116:5; Psalm 51:1; Psalm 119:77; Psalm 145:8; Isaiah 49:15; Isaiah 51:8 and 1 Peter 3:8.

61 Worthington, Everett. *Promoting Forgiveness in Clinical Practice*, Nov. 5 1997.

62 James Fowler's theory of faith development helps us understand that our images of God are appropriate for our stage of spiritual development. Our early years depend on the images we receive and experience, most of which are internalized with literal images. See Fowler's book *Stages of Faith*.

63 William and Kristi Gaultiere offer fourteen different images of God that persons have adopted into their belief system. See their book, *Mistaken Identity*.

Appendix

Suggested Readings Related to Forgiveness

Augsburg, David W. (1996). *Helping People Forgive*. Louisville: Westminster/John Knox Press.

Bergen, J & Schwan, S.M. (1985). *Forgiveness: A Guide to Prayer.* Winona, MN: Saint Mary's Press/Christian Brothers Publications.

Bonhoeffer, D. *Ethics.* (1955). London: SCM Press.

Bernardin, J. *The Gift of Peace.* (1977). Chicago: Loyola Press.
.
Brakenhielm, C.R. *Forgiveness.* (1993). Minneapolis: Augusburg/Fortress Press.

Carter, L. & Minirth, F. (1997). *The Choosing to Forgive Workbook.* Nashville: Thomas Nelson Publishers.

Casarjian, R. (1992). *Forgiveness: A Bold Choice for a Peaceful Heart.* New York: Bantam Books.

Cobb, J. Jr. (1995). *Grace and Responsibility: A Wesleyan Theology for Today.* Nashville: Abingdon Press.

Cochrane, L. *Forgiven and Set Free.* (1996). Grand Rapids: Baker Books.

Collins, K. J. (1998) *The Scripture Way of Salvation: The Heart of John Wesley's Theology.* Nashville: Abingdon Press.

DeYoung, C. P. (1997). *Reconciliation: Our Greatest Challenge - Our Only Hope.* Valley Forge: Judson Press.

Countryman, L.W. *Forgiven and Forgiving.* (1998). Harrisburg, PA.: Morehouse Publishing.

Enright, R. D., & J. North, (Eds.). (1998). *Exploring Forgiveness.* Madison, WI: University Wisconsin Press.

Gassin, E.A. & Wu, C. (1992). Forgiveness: A Developmental View. *Journal of Moral Education,* 21, 99-115.

Freedman, D. N. (Ed.). (1992). *The Anchor Bible Dictionary, Vol. 1-6.* New York: Doubleday.

Guthrie, U. (Ed.). (1997). To Forgive and To Be Forgiven, *Circuit Rider,* March, 1-26.

Hargrave, T.D. (1994). *Families and Forgiveness: Healing Wounds in the Intergenerational Family.* New York: Bruner/Mazel, Inc.

Hahn, W. (1994). Resolving Shame in Group Psychotherapy. *International Journal of Group Psychotherapy,* 44, 449-461.

Jones, L.G. (1995). *Embodying Forgiveness: A Theological Analysis.* Grand Rapids: William B. Eerdmans Publishing Company.

Klein, C. (1995). *How To Forgive When You Can't Forget.* Bellmore, N.Y.: Liebling Press.

Kohut, H. (1977) *The Restoration of the Self.* New York: International Universities Press

Kovach, K.K. (1994). *Mediation: Principles and Practice.* St. Paul: West Publishing Company.

Kushner, H. S. (1996). *How Good Do We Have to Be? A New Understanding of Guilt and Forgiveness.* New York: Beck Bay Books/Little, Brown and Company.

Lewis, H.B.(Ed.). (1987). *The Role of Shame in Symptom Formation.* Hildale, N.J.: Lawrence Erlbaum Associates.

Maddox, R. L. (1994). *Responsible Grace: John Wesley's s Practical Theology.* Nashville: Kingswood Books/Abingdon

McCullough, M. E. (1997). Marital Forgiveness: Theoretical Foundations and an Approach to Prevention. *Marriage and Family: A Christian Journal,* 1, 81-96.

McCullough, M.E., Sandage, S.. J. & Worthington, E. L., Jr. (1997*)* *To Forgive is Human: How To Put Your Past in the Past.* Downers Grove, IL.: InterVarsity Press.

McCullough, M. E. & Worthington, E. L. (1994). Models of Interpersonal Forgiveness and Their Applications to Counseling: Review and Critique. *Counseling and Values,* 39, 2-15.

Menninger, W.A. (1997). *The Process of Forgiveness.* New York: Continuum.

Menconi, P. & Clark, R. (1998). *Reconciling Relationships: Small Group Bible Studies .* Carol Stream, IL: Cross Trainers/Media Inc.

Moule, C.F. (1998). *Forgiveness & Reconciliation: Biblical and Theological Essays.* London: Society for Promoting Christian Knowledge.

Nathanson, D.L.(Ed.). (1987). *The Many Faces of Shame.* New York: Guilford Press.

Nouwen, H. (1994). *The Return of the Prodigal Son: A Story of Homecoming.* New York: Image Books/Doubleday.

Novotni, M. & Petersen, R. (2001). *Angry With God.*(Colorado Springs: Pinion Press.

Pingleton, J.P. (1997). Why We Don't Forgive: A Biblical and Object Relations Theoretical Model for Understanding Failures in the Forgiveness Process. *Journal of Psychology and Theology*, 25, 403-413.

Read, D. (Ed.). (1994). Forgiving, *The Living Pulpit*, 3 (2).

Schreiter, R.J. (1996). *Reconciliation: Mission and Ministry in A Changing Social Order*. Maryknoll, NY: Orbis Books.

Smalley, G. & Trent, J. (19986). *The Blessing*. New York: Pocket Books.

Smalley, G. & Trent, J. (1993). The Blessing Workbook. Nashville: Thomas Nelson Publishers.

Spero, M.H. (1984). Shame: An Object Relations Formulation. *The Psychoanalytic Study of the Child*, 39, 259-282.

Stokes, M. B. (1972). *Major United Methodist Beliefs*. Nashville: Abingdon Press.

Stoop, D. & Masteller, J. (1991). *Forgiving Our Parents, Forgiving Ourselves*. Ann Arbor, MI: Vine Press.

Volf, M. (1997). *Exclusion & Embrace: A Theological Exploration of Identity, Otherness and Reconciliation*. Nashville: Abingdon Press.

White, G. (1997, May 24). Spiritual Healing and Forgiveness, *The Atlanta Journal Constitution*, pp. F-2, F-4.

Worthington, E. L. & McCullough, M.E. (Eds.). (1998). *The Foundation of Forgiveness: Theories, Reviews, and Speculations About the Scientific Study of Forgiveness*. Radner, PA: The John Templeton Foundation Press.

Worthington, E.L. & DiBlasio, F.A. (1990) Promoting Mutual Forgiveness Within the Fractured Relationship. *Psychotherapy*, 27, 219-223.

Bibliography

Armstrong, K (1996). *In the Beginning.* New York: Alfred A. Knopf.

Arnold, J. C. (1997). *Seventy Times Seven: The Power of Forgiveness.* Farmington, Pa.: The Plough Publishing House/Bruderhof Foundation.

Bradshaw, J. (1988). *Healing the Shame that Binds You.* Deerfield Beach, FL: Health   Communications, Inc.

Brown, J. W. (Ed.). (1983). *The Martyred Chrisitian: 160 Readings from Dietrich Bonhoeffer.* New York: Collier/MacMillian.

Buber, M. (1952). *Good and Evil.* New York: Charles Scribners' Sons.

Brueggemann, W. (1982). *Genesis: The Interpretation Commentaries.* Atlanta: John Knox Press.

Brueggeman, W. (1993). *Praying the Psalms.* Winona, Minn.: Saint Mary's/Christian Brothers Publications.

Coyle, C. T. & Enright, R. D. (1997). Forgiveness Intervention With Post-Abortion Men. *Journal of Consulting and Clinical Psychology,* 65, 1042-1046.

Doka, K. J. (Ed.). (1989). *Disenfranchised Grief: Recognizing Hidden Sorrow.* Lexington, Mass, D.C. Heath & Co./ Lexington Books.

Dunham, M. (1978). *Workbook on Spiritual Disciplines.* Nashville, TN: The Upper Room.

Erikson, E. (1963). *Childhood and Society (2nd ed.).* New York: W.W. Horton & Co.

Flanigan, B. (1992). *Forgiving the Unforgivable: Overcoming the Bitter Legacy of Intimate Wounds.* New York: Macmillan Publishing Company

Flanigan, B. (1996). *Forgiving Yourself: A Step by Step Guide to Making Peace With Your Mistakes and Getting on With Your Life.* New York: Macmillan.

Fossom, M. A. and Marilyn J. M. (1989). *Facing Shame: Families in Recovery.* New York: W.W. Norton & Co.

Fowler, J. (1981). *Stages of Faith: The Psychology of Human Development and the Quest for Meaning.* San Francisco: Harper Collins.

Freedmon , S.R. & Enright, R.D. (1996). Forgiveness as the Intervention Goal with Incest Survivors. *Journal of Consulting and Clincial Psychology,* 64, 983-992.

Gaultiere, W. & Gaultiere, K. (1989). *Mistaken Identity.* Old Tappan, N.J.: Fleming H. Revell Co.

Kaufman, G. (1989). *The Psychology of Shame.* New York: Springer.

Kubler-Ross, E. (1969). *On Death and Dying.* New York: MacMillan.

Madanes, C. (1990). *Love, Sex and Violence.* New York: W.W. Norton and Co.

McCraty, R., Atkinson, M., Tiller, W., Rein, G., & Watkins, A. (1995). The Effects of Emotions on Short Term Power Spectrum Analysis on Heart Rate Variability. *American Journal of Cardiology,* 76, 1089-1093.

McCullough, M. E., Worthington, E. L., & Rachal, K. C. (1997). Interpersonal Forgiving in Close Relationships. *Journal of Personality and Social Psychology,* 73, 321-336.

143

Neeld, E. H. (1990). *Seven Choices: Taking the Steps to a New Life after Losing Someone You Love.* New York: Clarkson N. Potter, Inc.

Patton, J. (1985). *Is Human Forgiveness Possible?* (Nashville: Abingdon.

Patton, J. (2000) *"Forgiveness in Pastoral Care and Counseling."* In McCullough, M. E., Pargament, K. I., & Thoresen, C. E (Eds.), New York: The Guilford Press.

Peck, Scott M. (1983). *People of the Lie.* New York: Simon and Shuster.

Schell, D. W. (1990). *Getting Bitter or Getting Better.* St. Meinrad, IN: Abbey Press.

Schell, D. W. (1993). *Forgiveness Therapy.* St Meinrad, IN: Abbey Press.

Schneider, C. (1997). *Shame, Exposure and Privacy.* Boston: Beacon Press.

Smedes, *L. (1984). Forgive and Forget.* New York: Pocket Books.

Smedes, L. (1993). *Shame and Grace.* San Francisco: HarperSanFrancisco/Zondervan Publishing.

Smedes, L. (1996). *The Art of Forgiving.* Nashville: Moorings/ Ballantine

Steinbeck, J. (1952). *East of Eden.* New York: The Viking Press.

Telushkin, J. (1991). *Jewish Literacy.* New York: William Morrow & Co.

Tennen, H. & Affleck, G. (1990). Blaming Others for Threatening Events. *Psychology Bulletin, 108,* 209-232.

Trent and Smalley *(1986). The Blessing.* New York: Pocket Books.

Truong, K. T. (1991) *Human Forgiveness: A Phenomenological Study about the Process of Forgiveness.* Unpublished doctoral dissertation, U.S. International University, San Diego, CA Cited in McCullough, M.E., Pargament, K. I. & Thoresen, C. E. (eds.): *Forgiveness: Theory, Research and Practice.* New York: Guilford Press, 2000, 182.

Neufeldt, V. & Sparks, A. N. (Eds.). (1989). *Webster's New World Compact School and Office Dictionary,* New York: Simon and Schuster, Inc.

Worthington, E. L. (1997). *Promoting Forgiveness in Clinical Practice.* Paper presented at preconference workshop at the American Association of Christian Counselors World Conference on Christian Counseling, Dallas, TX.

Yancy, P. (1997). *What's So Amazing About Grace?* Grand Rapids: Zondervan Publishing House.

Booking Information

To schedule Dr. Ann O. Slimp and/or Dr. Bill Carpenter to host a workshop or seminar for your organization, or to speak at an event, please contact:

MMRi
1000 Peachtree Industrial Boulevard
Suite 6 – Box 309
Suwanee, Georgia 30024
770-831-7504

billcarpenter@mmri.info

aoslimp@mmri.info

or visit the MMRi Website at:

www.mmri.info

Yes! Please send a copy of *Forgiveness: An Invitation to Freedom.*

Just complete the information below and send to:

MMRi Publishing
1000 Peachtree Industrial Blvd., Suite 6 – 309
Suwanee, Georgia 30024

Quantity	Item	Cost
_____	Forgiveness: An Invitation to Freedom *($15.00 per copy)*	$_____
	Georgia residents add 6% sales tax	_____
	Shipping and handling	**$2.50**
	Total Cost	$_____

Name _____ Phone (_____) _____

Address _____

City _____ St _____ Zip _____

Payment Method: ☐ Visa   ☐ MasterCard   ☐ Check (payable to **MMRi**)

Credit Card Information:

Visa/MC Number _____ Exp. _____/_____

Name on Card _____

Cardholder Signature _____

(770) 831-7504   •   www.mmri.info

Evaluation

(You can also use the MMRi website to complete an evaluation
of *Forgiveness: An Invitation to Freedom.*)

Please take a moment to complete this evaluation form and return it to:

MMRi Publishing
1000 Peachtree Industrial Blvd., Suite 6 – 309
Suwanee, Georgia, 30024

[1] Not very helpful [2] Somewhat helpful
[3] Moderately helpful [4] Very Helpful [5] Extremely Helpful

How would you rate this book? ☐ 1 ☐ 2 ☐ 3 ☐ 4 ☐ 5

Please identify the most helpful section and offer comments:

_____

_____

Please identify the least helpful section and offer any comments?

_____

_____

How would you rate the study guides? ☐ 1 ☐ 2 ☐ 3 ☐ 4 ☐ 5

Comments? _____

_____

Would you like us to send you additional information about forgiveness
seminars? ☐ Yes ☐ No

Name _____

Address _____

City _____ St ____ Zip _____

E-mail _____

Your Story

We have been inspired by many of the people we have met through our classes and workshops on forgiveness. By applying the principles in this book, many people have forgiven and been reconciled with persons who were once completely distant and alienated. We would invite you to share your forgiveness story with us. Although there is a place to include your name and address, we invite anonymous stories as well. All information will be treated in confidence unless you specifically indicate that your story could be shared as an example to others.

Name _____

Address _____

City _____ St ____ Zip _____

E-mail _____

Dr. William Carpenter is a United Methodist Minister and holds degrees from Lambuth University, Florida State University, Emory University, State University of West Georgia, and Columbia Theological Seminary. Bill and his wife Gayle live in Suwanee, Georgia.

Dr. Ann O'Connor-Slimp is a Licensed Psychologist in Tennessee. She has served as a therapist and teacher for a number of years. Ann received her undergraduate degree from the State University of West Georgia and her Ph.D. in psychology from Auburn University. Ann and her husband Kevin have two children, Ashley and Zachary. They live in Knoxville.